The Treatment of Chemical Dependency with Clinical Hypnotherapy

The Treatment of Chemical Dependency with Clinical Hypnotherapy

Randy J. Hartman, M. A.

Writers Club Press
San Jose New York Lincoln Shanghai

The Treatment of
Chemical Dependency with Clinical Hypnotherapy

Writers Club Press
an imprint of iUniverse.com, Inc.

For information address:
iUniverse.com, Inc.
620 North 48th Street, Suite 201
Lincoln, NE 68504-3467
www.iuniverse.com

ISBN: 0-595-14699-6

Printed in the United States of America

Contents

INTRODUCTION

The decision to write this book came from many of my students who were Chemical Dependency Counselors. They pointed out to me that were no clear and concise books available on the market that dealt with clinical hypnotherapy and chemical dependency treatment in a well integrated and usable manner for the therapist.

What makes this book different from the many texts already on the market dealing with the subject of treating chemical dependency is the integrated involvement of clinical hypnosis. Until now the use of hypnosis with addictions has been generally used with nicotine and food addictions.

The time is overdue to bring clinical hypnosis out of the closet and into the chemical dependency treatment arena. While clinical hypnosis will not be the saving grace in the area of chemical dependency, it will certainly become a very strong adjunctive therapy. The term "hypnosis" still conjures up visions of evil and manipulation for many people that have never had any formal training in the subject.

Hypnosis training for a licensed counselor need only be twenty-four hours to start with. Licensed Addictions Counselors already have the required counseling background so this allows for a short, and rapid training to start using clinical hypnotherapy in their counseling practice.

It is time, matter of fact, long overdue for the use of clinical hypnosis again in therapy. The use of clinical hypnotherapy has a long and very extensive history. The military used it widely during WWII and following that period some texts appeared during the late forties and early fifties on the subject of treating alcoholics and drug addicts, but were quickly forgotten. Now society has found new value in treating the chemically addicted and the time is right to add clinical hypnosis to the treatment arsenal of the Addictions Counselor.

It is my hope that you will find this book to be a very usable desktop reference for your treatment of the chemically dependent.

THE HISTORY OF CLINICAL HYPNOSIS AND ADDICTIONS

As we start with a look into the past at the use of clinical hypnosis with chemical dependency we will only go back as far as 1949. In an old journal titled "Hypnotism Today", LeCron and Bordeaux provided reference to treating drug addicts. Dr Van Pelt in 1958 referred to treating alcoholics with hypno-analysis. He referred to the viscious cycle created by alcoholism and pointed out the extreme importance of finding the root cause of the neurosis that is responsible for alcoholism. In 1961 Dr William Bryan developed a system of treating alcoholics with what he called the basic five R's of hypnotic treatment: Relaxation, realization, re-education, rehabilitation and reinforcement.

Bryan's first R was relaxation. This was just simply relaxation, or sometimes known as the Hypnodial State. He felt the patient could communicate better with the therapist from this state.

The second R represented realization. Bryan felt that the patient must be made to realize the main cause of his drinking behavior. Bryan expressed his feelings that the individual cause for drinking was always multiple. This always called for age regression back to the very first time the person took a drink and every subsequent problem experience associated with drinking. With each problem re-visited the person would usually experience a catharsis that he needed. Then the negative emotions associated with each event were removed.

R number three was re-education. This is how the patient was shown the relationship between his drinking behavior and the underlying causes. A change of attitude towards problems and stress in his life must also be addressed. This phase will be complete when the patient's compulsion is gone and catharsis is completed.

Rehabilitation represents the fourth R. Bryan contends that the true rehabilitation of the alcoholic consists of breaking the habit pattern and strengthening the ego. The habit pattern can be broke in two ways, either by eliminating it entirely, or by substituting another habit pattern for the existing one.

Bryan stressed the fact that unless the compulsion to drink has been completely taken care of in the first three steps of this process, the substitution of a new habit pattern will not be sufficient to deter the alcoholic from drinking.

The fifth R of Bryan's system of hypnotic treatment is reinforcement. This phase consists of seeing the alcoholic at regular intervals after the completion of hypnotherapy proper for the reinforcement of suggestions previously administered. Bryan does stress over and over again to individualize the treatment of alcoholics and drug addicts.

Bryan claimed to have a ninety percent success rate with this treatment approach. I have attempted to research more information on Bryan's five Rs and his reported success rate and could turn up no further information.

Kroger (19631) reported the results in small groups were often better than with individual hypnotherapy in the treatment of alcoholics. The group met weekly with a two-hour session. Each session was conducted in three phases.

Phase one of the session begins with a general discussion of alcoholism in which questions and answers are addressed. Education of the patient seems to be the main thrust of phase one. Also during phase one patients share with the group any particular problems they may be currently faced with.

Phase two consists of having one or more of the successful patients describe how well they are doing and how learning self-hypnosis has facilitated great improvements in their life. What this accomplishes is having a "successful" role model speak out in-group to raise a considerable amount of hope with the other group members.

The final group phase, phase three consists of teaching the patients self-hypnosis. Along with teaching the patients autohypnosis the therapist also helps the patients develop a strong aversion to alcohol. The patients are given suggestions to not drink along with sensory images that should produce a profound disgust to the taste and smell of alcohol. Kroger also suggests that each patient be allowed to select his own sensory images. With the incorporation of auto-hypnosis coupled with the patient's own sensory adverse images, the patient then directs and takes more responsibility for his own recovery.

Now we can take a quick look at past intervention with drug addicts. In 1967 Bryan reported limited success working with the hardcore drug addict. However, he reported good results with these cases provided that the following conditions were present:

The patient himself must be well motivated in order for him to have any lasting benefits. The patient must be under constant supervision. The drug supply must be completely and permanently shut off from the patient. Also an extensive hypno-anaylsis must be done to uncover every significant neurosis, and direct suggestion must be given which will afford the patient new escape values to replace the use of the drug of choice.

Most important, the patient must be seen a minimum of one or two hours daily until a complete cure is effected, and then hypnotic suggestions should continue until one is positively assured that recurrence is unlikely.

Hypnosis has also been seen as an aversion form of therapy. Truman (1971) traumatized a drug addict against any use of a needle. After the patient went through her withdrawal period the posthypnotic suggestion was given that she was to be normal in all respects, but that if she or anyone else attempted to put a needle into her body at any place, she would have a violent physical reaction. Then before bringing her back out from trance she was also told she would not consciously remember that this suggestion had been given to her. Truman reported that she attempted to shoot up drugs within a week and became violently ill when the needle pierced her arm.

Kroeger (1963) felt that autohypnosis was especially helpful for withstanding the disagreeable sensations produced by withdrawal. During the withdrawal phase he suggested that the addict use sensory-imagery conditioning to imagine that he is giving himself an injection or taking a drug orally while in hypnosis. The thought behind this is when the patient can revivify the pleasurable effects of the drug, withdrawal is accomplished more readily.

A rather interesting technique was described by Baumann (1970) in which he used the following steps with adolescent drug abusers with excellent success.

Baumann first provided a complete history and physical examination with a sincere attempt at establishing rapport, reliving of a previous "good trip" or happy drug experience. He had the patient develop the hallucinated drug experience into one which in the patient's opinion was more rewarded, more intense than the original trip.

Baumann felt that the advantages of such an approach are that self-induced hallucinated experiences are not against the law, they are free and totally under the subject's control, and thus provide the freedom he need for independence, without depriving the person of the kick, adventure or escape previously supplied by the injection or ingestion of illegal or expensive drugs with unpredictable present or future effects.

In the past many approaches were attempted with clinical hypnosis to treat the chemically dependent. Some approaches were more radical that others, while most can be nearly described as traditional. There is a definite strong need for more on going well documented research with clinical hypnotherapy and the chemically dependent. There are a wide array of approaches available for the treatment of the chemically dependent. The most accepted school of thought in the field of chemical dependency in the late 1980s to present is the "disease concept". Regardless of what school of thought you may choose to subscribe to, clinical hypnotherapy can become a valuable asset in the treatment of the chemically dependent.

Training in clinical hypnotherapy is available for chemical dependency counselors' nationwide. Average initial training is usually twenty-four hours. As of this date only California and New York require testing to register as a Clinical Hypnotherapist. The initial training can occur in a short period of time, such as twenty-four hours if the person being trained is already a trained counselor/therapist. The need to learn the basic counseling skills has already been satisfied and the individual can readily grasp the material presented. Continuing education in clinical hypnotherapy is a real must for any counselor/therapist who desires to excel with the use of hypnosis.

For those Chemical Dependency Counselors who will go on to pursue training in the field of clinical hypnotherapy, I would urge you to carefully select the training you take. Check with your state chemical dependency counselor certification board to see if they recognize the trainer and course material presented.

Denial, Defeating the Little Monster

Once the patient is detoxified, the next obvious hurdle to overcome is usually denial. The problem of denial is interlaced throughout the very life fiber of the chemically dependent individual and their lifestyle. They generally refuse and will go to great lengths to avoid accepting any responsibility for their behaviors.

This denial seems at times to be a nearly indestructible vault constructed of a combination of psychological defense mechanisms and the effects which sustain the addict. This also includes altered perceptions, dissociation, and memory blackouts. As long as systems continue to operate, the more the chemically dependent become more out of touch with reality. It is truly amazing that while the individual is going through all of this that he often appear to be completely rational. A few of the hallmark personality traits that usually appear with the chemically dependent are immaturity, demanding of others and dependent on others.

Denial can be seen on the conscious level with an individual refusing to accept responsibility. Denial can also be seen on the unconscious level.

This is known as compliance. This can be best described as a person appearing to have given up his defenses and accepting his addiction, while actually continuing to believe that does not have a problem. Compliance is seen in large quantity with those patients that check in for treatment because of pressure from legal referrals, spouses, jobs, etc. Until there is total surrender, denial in one form or another will continuously get in the way of total wellness. When doing trance work or any therapy, I always replace the word "surrender" with the word "acceptance". The word "surrender" has a negative connotation to it, implying the person is giving up self-control, and no one wants to do that. I see using the word "surrender" as a quick way to set up resistance with the patient, at least on a subconscious level.

The more standard approach to dealing with denial has been confrontation. The patient is confronted by his counselor, spouse, and peers in an attempt to get the person to accept that he has a problem with alcohol/drugs. Even the legal system confronts the patient and orders him to treatment. The majority of the patients I have dealt with in the past often appear to surrender, but in reality shift to the compliance mode. In the compliance mode they find the payoff of getting positive strokes from others as they appear to be taking responsibility for their actions. These patients are often very good actors and smooth talkers, able to manipulate others at a moments notice.

Now that the problem is identified, what kind(s) of hypnotic intervention can we use to move the chemically dependent patient past the compliance mode? Possibly the best place to begin is with hypno-analysis of the patient. Hypno-analysis is doing analysis, but under the influence of hypnosis.

With the given situation, it would be best to start the hypno-analysis with age regressing the patient back to his first incident of drinking to intoxication. It is an interesting phenomenon that those clients who are chemically dependent can easily recall their first time of drinking to intoxication, and describe every detail that transpired. On the other hand, those not chemically dependent usually have a great deal of difficulty recalling their first event! I have come to view this phenomenon as the alcoholic reviving the "birth" of their drinking because it is viewed by them on some level as a significant event.

Once you have age regressed them back to that point in time of their first intoxication, have them slowly recall everything that was said and done, especially recalling the feeling surrounding the drinking/using event. Continue talking at that level so they process all the events and feelings associated with the event. With many of these events you can anticipate a catharsis as the patient grieves the event.

This process should continue to cover all the major drinking events. Other drinking events will be remembered by the patient, but the major events are the ones you and the patient should focus on. After the patient completes the initial hypno-analytic event, they will usually be able to continue to move forward in time. If the patient seems to be stuck or reluctant to move forward, it will be necessary to process that event even deeper and clear up any unfinished business.

This may seem like an extremely long and drawn out process to take a patient through, but it really is not an overwhelming task when you consider that you and the patient are dealing primarily with the major drinking/using events. Time is normally on your side, after the patient probably has invested years in developing his addiction. The best possibly educated guess I could offer in a time frame with hypno-analysis would be using the example of a middle stage alcoholic with a twelve year addiction history. The time frame I would presuppose would be approximately eighteen sessions devoted to hypno-analysis. The variables are unlimited, but most middle stage patients are seen in an alcohol & drug outpatient setting for a minimum of one year or more, allowing for adequate treatment time.

To accurately discriminate between the states of denial, compliance, and acceptance can be a very difficult task. Most addictions counselors I have spoken on this subject explain that they can discern fairly accurately, but on an intuitive level. Confrontation of the patient seems to be the normal course of action by counselors when they believe a patient is in only a compliance mode. From my experience, and the experience related to me from other addictions specialists, I have found it to be largely non-pro-ductive to confront a patient when your only basis is your intuition. Without real evidence you have no way to hold the patient's "feet to the fire" for change.

Hypno-analysis is one possible way of breaking through denial and compliance. Another possibility would be negotiating between parts of the subconscious to bring the patient to the stage of acceptance. The late great Virginia Satir was a great pioneer in the area of negotiating between subconscious parts. Neuro Linguistic Programming (NLP) went on to better shape and formalize procedures for negotiating between parts of the subconscious.

The following will be a sample script of negotiating between parts of the subconscious as we try to arrive at the stage of acceptance with a mid-dle stage alcoholic. The first step is to take the patient into trance to the state of somnambulism to begin the work.

SAMPLE SCRIPT

As you continue to relax and enjoy the special place you have created for yourself, I would like to ask your conscious mind to remain there while I talk with your subconscious mind. Allow your conscious mind to watch TV or just enjoy your special place while I talk with your subconscious mind. I would now like to talk to the subconscious part that controls his ability to have acceptance of his alcoholism, and ask you to tell me what your positive function is? (Listen for response, repeat the question if necessary) What part is getting in the way of you doing your job? Now I would like to communicate with that part of your subconscious that controls his compliance, and ask you to tell me your positive function is? (Listen for response, are parts blocking each other?) Would the part of your subconscious that controls his compliance be willing to not interfere with his part that controls his acceptance of alcoholism, if the part that controls his acceptance will not get in the way of you doing your job? (Notice answer) Now I would like to ask your subconscious parts to agree to this deal for at least six months (Notice response). Are there any other parts of your subconscious affected by this agreement? (Notice response) (Now rejoin conscious and subconscious).

Now to look back and examine what has happened. In trance we have negotiated a time specific agreement between the subconscious parts of acceptance and compliance. The timeline needs to be established in sufficient length to allow the new behavior to become routine for the patient as the old behavior fades away during the Sufficient specified time. Just what is the minimum amount of time needed for this to occur is debatable by many professionals. I have always found great success with using the timeline of six months.

By negotiating with the subconscious we have bypassed the conscious mind and deal directly only with the "Boss", the subconscious. Nothing happens with our behavior that doesn't first originate in the subconscious. So anytime we take our interventions to the "Boss", we can expect better results. The mired conscious can get in the way with its defense system.

The next possibility we can look at for helping patients gain the state of acceptance is to create a new part in subconscious. With some patients it will seem hopeless to try and locate a part in the subconscious that will take responsibility for the acceptance behavior. In reality we are not creating something entirely new in the subconscious.

First, initiate a trance and deepen to somnambulism. Have the patient access any historical experience of (acceptance), or anything similar. Step inside each experience and access all aspects of (acceptance). Go through each memory in all representational systems, visual, feelings and auditory.

Now create a detailed set of images of how you would behave if you were actually demonstrating whatever this part of you is going to have you to do to achieve the outcome.

Next create a dissociated visual and auditory constructed movie. Ask the patient the following: When you see a whole sequence that you are satisfied with, step inside the images and go through the whole sequence again from the inside, feeling what It is like to do these new behaviors. If you are not satisfied, go back and reconstruct the movie. Do this until you are satisfied with that fantasy from the inside as well as from the outside, making all the sights and sounds very bright and vivid.

At this time ask if there are any subconscious parts that object to having this new part. Satisfy any objections that maybe found. Once complete ask the new part to run through the constructed movie. Terminate or deepen trance.

Now that the procedure is completed we can see that nothing really new has been added to the subconscious, but old information is reassimilated. With this new part the subconscious has a new point of reference to refer to when acceptance is sought. Throughout this intervention we are keeping the patient empowered by using his resources stored in his mind. Now the patient is properly empowered with the information and a point of reference to better deal with the issue of acceptance.

Another possible therapeutic tool for your arsenal can be accomplished by using "Cherval's Pendulum". As most of us already know, Cherval's Pendulum procedure is basically a hypnotic suggestibility test. Some veteran hypnotherapists will no doubt scoff at this idea immediately, but I would like to urge you to bear with me as I explain. For those readers not readily familiar with Cherval's Pendulum, I will take a moment to elaborate on it before moving on with my explanation.

Cherval's Pendulum was developed by a French pharmacist and widely used as a hypnotic suggestibility test, and also widely thought of as the forerunner of the Ouija board. To construct Cherval's pendulum use a thread, chain or string about ten inches long. To this string you can attach a key, paperclip or ball. The next step is to draw a circle about eight inches in diameter on a piece of paper. Then draw two intersecting lines through the circle, from top to bottom and left to right. Then label the left side with the word "true", and the right side with the word "false". Next label the topside as "maybe" and the bottom as "don't know".

Once constructed have the patient hold the string and paper clip over the center of the paper with his elbow resting on the table. Now instruct the patient to say the following: "Am I just being compliant about my treatment?" If he is being just compliant the pendulum will swing towards true. This will provide you good information with which to confront the patient with. The subconscious will respond in the form of involuntary muscle movement. This procedure can be quite accurate as long as you do not give the patient prior exposure, such as the opportunity to play with the pendulum as the patient could figure out how to manipulate it.

For those readers that tend to scoff and dismiss this procedure, I recommend you allow yourself to try it at least once with a patient. Then make your judgment based on the outcome. I believe many therapists will be pleasantly surprised with the results. There are an unlimited number of possibilities with clinical hypnotherapy to assist your patients in working through the stages of denial, compliance and acceptance. Clinical hypnotherapy is a wonderful adjunctive tool.

CRAVING, GOTTA HAVE IT

For some chemically dependent patients in the early stages of recovery, their drug of choice is a very real and threatening problem. For other patients this can seem to not be a problem for them at all. There already are a variety of interventions frequently used that seem to work quite well for craving. Unfortunately not all patients are the same, their perceptions and needs vary greatly. Every patient's model of the world varies from one another. So we must sometimes "tailor" interventions to meet their particular model of the world.

In the following pages I will offer a variety of possible hypnotic interventions to assist your patients with that "gotta have it," mindset we know as craving their drug of choice. First we aim at something as simple as symptom substitution. An example might be substituting the craving for the taste of raw carrots in place of the craving for the taste of alcohol. Whatever is used to substitute needs to be specific. To tell the patient they will crave raw vegetables is not specific enough. It would be better to assign a specific vegetable in a specific form, i.e., the example of the raw carrots.

Before attempting symptom substitution it would be wise to take into account the patient's "model of the world". They may find the taste of raw carrots unacceptable. Possible the best way to approach this is to have a dialogue with your patient and ask them to choose the substitute. Over the years I have found that the majority of my patients will select something as simple as water. To install the symptom substitution you first need to take the patient into trance and then install the substitution in the form of a post-hypnotic suggestion. Repeat this suggestion at least three times or more. If possible build the suggestion using a higher order of complexity.

Beyond symptom substitution we will now look at disassociation as a means to alleviate craving with a patient. Disassociation will teach the patient to disassociate, move away from the craving when it occurs. When the craving occurs their mind goes elsewhere. It is important that when you devise the form of disassociation for the patient that you utilize whatever the patient's model of the world will find acceptable. If the patient can not relate to the context of the disassociation, their subconscious will void or limit the effectiveness.

In trance the disassociation is installed by using a post-hypnotic suggestion. The principle of disassociation is that when the patient's mind starts to focus on the craving, his mind will automatically shift to a different, more positive thought. An example of what the suggestion may sound like might be: The next time your craving for (drug of choice) you will find your thoughts automatically will change to reciting the alphabet from beginning to end.

Here again just a reminder, for this procedure to work effectively for your patient you need to ensure that the disassociation will be acceptable in your patient's model of the world. The example cited above would proba-bly work for a patient who was an English major, writer, or schoolteacher.

Another interesting possibility in treating the patient's craving for their drug of choice could be the use of the "Swish Pattern". Nuero Linguistic Programming uses this procedure for an array of problems. It is also another basic form of allowing the patient to disassociate. To employ the Swish Pattern with a patient I offer the following outline:

1. Before trance, ask the patient to vividly recall the craving and feel-ings associated with it.

2. Ask the patient to create a wonderful peaceful picture in his mind, complete with all the good feelings.

3. Now take the patient into trance to the state of somnambulism. Instruct the patient to see a blank movie screen in their mind's eye. Instruct the patient to visualize the craving scene on the blank movie screen. Now have the patient take the nice image and place it in one corner of the movie screen. Ask the patient to now allow the nice pic-ture to grow and rapidly over take the craving scene. Have the patient repeat this twice more, covering the craving scene in two seconds or less. Once accomplished the procedure is done.

To test what you have done, after trance ask your patient to recall the craving scene. The patient should not be able to readily reca11 that picture without the nice picture overtaking it. Depending on your patient, you may need to focus more on feelings than visual effects. Possibly you may need to build more on taste and smell instead of the visual field of representation.

Autohypnosis is yet another possible method for assisting the patient in early recovery with craving. Since the craving for the patient's drug of choice seems to mainly occur during the early stages of recovery, you will need to evaluate if your patient is in a good state of mind to learn self-hypnosis. With self-hypnosis the patient can become empowered to self-regulate his ability to disassociate or minimize his discomfort with his craving as well as other problems that would be common to early recovery.

In a few sessions the patient can learn to self induce trance very quickly to resolve problems. Along with teaching your patients how to self hypnotize, it is critical to also teach the patients how to form their own curative suggestions to work on their specific problems, I believe the more we can empower our patients, the greater the odds become for them to be able to maintain a state of healthy recovery. For more extensive information on autohypnosis I would recommend another book I have written entitled, "The Key to Hypnosis".

A strong support system for the chemically dependent patient is also a must. If the patient feels as though he is losing his self-control, he needs a readily available support system. Beyond the therapist the best possible support system would be AA or NA. Family and friends are also a good support system, but if the patient feels that there are some things he is not comfortable talking about with them, then the patient should have at his disposal a current list of AA or NA meetings in the community, and hopefully a sponsor.

CO-DEPENDENCY, THE SIGNIFICANT OTHERS

Codependency is a very vogue term that really becomes very vague in its entirety. This term codependency can seem to apply to everyone in its general definition. Usually it is used to refer to the spouses of chemically dependent persons, their children, those people who have a strong urge to act as caretakers or rescuers of other people or people who have problems establishing healthy boundaries. The list could go on and on, but in this book the word codependency will refer to the psychological, emotional, physical, social, and other related problems that arise as the direct result of being in a close relationship with a chemically dependent person.

Since this book is aimed at a target audience of chemical dependency counselors, I will not go into any elaborate detail about the family systems and the roles assumed by those close to the chemically dependent. The intent of this chapter is to explore possible hypnotic interventions with those persons in a close relationship with a chemically dependent person. The types of problems seen with the significant others are without limits.

To leave the significant others out of the treatment process is almost pre-destining the patient to extreme difficulties, if not outright failure.

In the pursuit of treating codependency we must also understand one of the most common addictions, love. Addictive love can be very exciting and seductive. Love addicts always seem to fall "madly in love" with the other person. They become very "crazy" about that special someone and try to make that individual theirs. Love addicts will normally treat the person they love like a substance and become compulsively preoccupied with getting, maintaining, and using a supply of him or her. After awhile, being with the object of their affection no longer feels as good as it first did, but if they try to end to relationship, they find that they cannot stay away from that person. At this point they have started to experience tolerance and withdrawal. Love addiction can create an extremely dysfunctional relationship and is a very powerful contributor to a phenomenon such as domestic violence and divorce.

Addiction to love is bad enough by itself, but even worse is the addiction love with a chemically dependent person. This condition is what is meant here by codependency. A codependent person is obsessed with and dependent on a chemically dependent person, who in turn is obsessed with and dependent on chemicals. Codependent people often complain about the addicted person's addiction, but they also enable the addiction by supplying the chemicals or rescuing and protecting the addicted person when they get into trouble. Often they have a vested interest in keeping the addiction going so that the addicted person will be disabled and there-fore need them. This ensures their continued supply of the addicted person's time and attention.

With this information as a backdrop, we can now look forward to examining various possible interventions with the significant others of the chemically dependent. In most situations these codependent patients are treated in a group setting. For some treatment centers with a large volume of chemically dependent patients, the group setting for their significant others is the only practical approach considering the sheer numbers to deal with. The group approach can be quite functional and especially good for providing these significant others an educational format. We cannot expect positive change in people until we educate them.

From the hypnotic perspective, managing a group can be much more difficult to deal with effectively that dealing with them one on one. You need to organize a well regimented codependency program that includes a requirement for individual and group counseling for the clientele. During the individual sessions the patient can be exposed and conditioned to trance work, and if all the group members are conditioned the same, then group therapy with hypnosis will be much more effective. Without the conditioning you will have group members at all various stages of trance and some patients will be deep enough for an intervention while others are not.

One possible issue that can be addressed in the early stages of a program is self-esteem. The issue of self worth is normally a large issue with the codependent who is used to feeding off the chemically dependent person to gain their self-worth and ego strength. In a group setting the codependent could be taken into a trance and simple ego building suggestions used, or perhaps metaphors. The codependent person needs to learn to understand that they have a separate identity of their own that they can be proud of. Those codependents that reach a conclusion that they are there in treatment for themselves, and not to rescue their chemically dependent significant others are the people that will move forward to success. Unfortunately a large these codependents will initially become resistant to engage in treatment for themselves.

The range of problems presented by the codependent person could be virtually anything from sexual abuse to obsessive-compulsive behavior to all points in between. As a therapist your primary strength will be drawn from your ability to be creative and flexible as you tailor the interventions to fit your patient's model of the world.

Autohypnosis for your motivated codependent patient can be a true asset for them. The reason I specified motivated patients is because they will need their own personal motivation to practice self-hypnosis on their own. If there is no practice, then there is no positive payoff for the patient. There are a few different approaches to teaching patients self-hypnosis, the long way and the short way.

The long way to teach patients self-hypnosis is to formally teach the patient the mechanics and various methods of inducing self-hypnosis. Instructionally this may take anywhere from three to five hours. The shorter method I have come to prefer is teaching the patient from their trance experience. Once the patient has been hypnotized two or more times they have established a point of reference as to what trance feels like for them. With this ready point of reference the patient has knowledge to draw upon to recall these feeling of trance for themselves independent of the therapist. To facilitate this I would give the patient a post-hypnotic suggestion that when they squeeze their thumb and index finger together they can vividly recall those feelings of trance. All that is left to do is to teach the patient how to construct their own curative suggestions. I have found that most patients in the beginning are not interested in all the fine details of self-hypnosis; perhaps this could be taught later. Some therapists prefer to provide their patients with a cassette tape to use on their own.

HYPNOTIC INTERVENTIONS FOR THE CHEMICALLY DEPENDENT

During this chapter we will examine numerous interventions that can be used to treat your patients and the problems they present. The interventions in this chapter will not only deal specifically with drinking and drugging behavior, but also interventions for the wide array of problems the patients will present with just because they are human beings.

The other issues we will also address and deal with, such as phobias, PTSD, unresolved past issues, grief issues, self-esteem, weight loss, and nicotine addiction. This will probably be the one chapter that you refer back to most often in your daily practice.

Effective interventions for the chemically dependent depend largely on the creativity of the therapist and your understanding of the patient's model of the world. Having a clear understanding of your patient's model of the world is something I cannot emphasize enough. While many of these interventions will work just fine as they are written for some of your patients, I would recommend you approach these interventions as model frameworks. Do not hesitate to add or subtract and alter these interventions to meet the needs of your patients.

If you have done a complete and in-depth intake interview with your patient you will have sufficient information to start working with their model of the world. Another point worth mentioning here is that if your patient isn't "broke" there is no intervention strong enough to "fix it". Occasionally we need to remind ourselves as therapists to allow our patients to assign their own priorities to their problems, not our priorities to their problems. Some patients want to give us a smaller problem at first to see if we can handle it before handing us their number one problem and as I stated before, whatever works in their model of the world. Now lets move on to the interventions.

Hypnotic Antabuse

This is a form of hypnotic aversion therapy that applies to all habits, alcohol, drug, tobacco, etc.

Possible Uses:

Adults who have been medically denied Antabuse.

Adolescents, 13 to 19 years old.

There must be some expressed desire to abstain.

Do Not Use:

If the patient has a bleeding ulcer.

If the patient refuses to consent.

To Install:

Post-hypnotic suggestion.

Describe the desired reaction in detail.

Reinforce 2-3 times during trance.

Follow-up at least once weekly and reinforce as needed.

Safety Feature:

The suggestion will be voided by the subconscious if the individual should start to approach a state of danger to their health. Beware that some patients will try to test the potency of the suggestion by using their drug of choice.

AGE PROGRESSION

This procedure has also been dubbed "Success Therapy". By taking the patient to the future he can see himself doing all the right things at the correct time in the proper sequence. Basically it is a rehearsal of a behavior in the future. This establishes an association of the familiarity of a desired response within a specific context.

Induction

Build a response set and use "future tense" in the hypnotic patter to move your patient's mind into the future mode.

Use metaphors and analogies regarding the future. Design and use a metaphor to talk about positive future changes.

Identify positive resources, with your hypnotic patter reinforce the patient's ability to learn, adapt and change.

Identify specific future contexts. Verbally review the specific situation(s) in a future context.

Embedding positive resources. Standard resource models would be learning, opportunities, loving, caring and adapting.

Rehearse behavioral sequence. Incorporate those positive words while having the patient see himself doing the task easily and competently in specific situations. Allow the patient to have the subjective experience of having weeks and months of rehearsal within a single session by distorting time.

Generalization of resources. Ask the patient to see himself in other specific situation(s). Allow about one minute of silence for the patient to complete the task.

Post-hypnotic suggestion. Form a single and non-complex suggestion that the patient can take this new understanding with them into his life. Terminate trance.

SWISH PATTERN

This procedure is multi-purpose in nature. It can apply to drinking, smoking, nail biting, PTD, and almost any habit.

1. Verify trance state.

2. Ask the client to recall the undesired pictures/situation as if they were watching a movie screen. Install ideomoter signaling.

3. Have them run the picture on the movie screen up to the worst part (apex) and signal you when it occurs.

4. At this point, ask the client to "freeze" that picture on the screen.

5. Instruct the patient to visualize a nice, wonderful image in one corner of the screen.

6. Then tell them that the nice scene is starting to grow, and slowly allow it to grow and over take the negative picture (Be patient and slowly talk them through it).

7. Ecology check. After trance ask the client to recall the negative picture and observe for any reactions. If a reaction is still present, then you may need to reinforce the technique.

CHANGING PERSONAL HISTORY

The purpose is to establish a new emotional association to an old memory. This might be especially good for patients with unresolved abuse issues from their childhood or any other past trauma.

1. Induction

2. Response set
    a. Asking the patient to think about his life the way it has been.
    b. Now ask the patient to think about it his life the way he wanted it to be.

3. Age regression to a specific event
    a. Ideomoter signal when event is clearly recalled.

4. Facilitate verbalization of context.
    a. Verbalize content with client.
    b. Identify specific resources needed to change the context of the event.

5. Re-experience context of event with additional resources needed to have a positive outcome.
    a. Amplify and associate feelings and images of the new outcome to the old event.

6. Validate and facilitate integration of the change.
    a. Verify positive feelings.
    b. Validate positive self-image with the new change.

Six Step Reframe, Modified

This NLP intervention is a good all around tool for dealing with habits. The procedure allows the patient to draw upon their own internal resources to reach an effective outcome to their presenting problem. With your patient arriving at their own decisions that fit their model of the world they are more likely to find success.

Identify behavior to be changed.
EXAMPLE: I want to stop smoking, but can't. I want to be a non-smoker but something stops me.

Induce trance; take patient to a working state.

Separate the conscious from the subconscious state.

Install ideomoter signaling, one for yes, and two for no.

Ask the part to communicate with you: "Will the part of (name) subconscious that, allows him to smoke communicate with me?"

Notice response (yes/no).

Thank the part for communicating.

Verify that the part is the subconscious: " Is this the subconscious part that controls (name) smoking behavior?"

Once this second verification is complete, again thank the part for communicating with you.

Ask the question; "Are you willing to let me know what your positive function/intention is?" Ask the patient to state the positive intention.

Notice response, thank the part for communicating.

If there were ways to accomplish your positive function that would work as well as or better than the present (behavior to be changed) would you be interested in trying them out?

If you get a no response, proceed with the reframing, presupposing a positive intention.

Access the creative part; " Will the creative part of (name) communicate with me?" Notice response.

Ask the creative part to generate at least three new and acceptable alternative behaviors that work as good or better than the unwanted behavior. Ask the patient to signal "Yes" when each new behavior is arrived at.

Future pace: Are you willing to take responsibility for using the three new alternatives in an appropriate context? Notice response, if no or no response, return to searching for new alternatives. Thank the creative part for its cooperation.

Ecology check: Are there any parts that object to the new alternatives? Notice response, if yes return to the creative part for other alternatives. If parts still object then negotiate between parts.

Closing Frame: Thank all the parts for their cooperation and participation. Ask the conscious mind to rejoin.

If the undesired behavior returns in the future, repeat the process as soon as possible.

Negotiating Between Parts

With this procedure you can assist your patient in over coming those mental blocks that get in the way of making an effective behavioral change, i.e. drinking, smoking, etc.

1. Ask the part that is being interrupted (part X) the following questions:
   a. What is your positive function?
   b. Which part(s) is (are) interrupting you? (part Y)

2. Ask the same questions of Y:
   a. What is your positive function?
   b. Does X ever interfere with your carrying out your function?

3. If both parts interrupt each other at times you are now ready to negotiate an agreement. (If not, this model is not appropriate.

Switch to another reframing model. If Y interferes with X, but X doesn't interfere with Y, a six-step reframe might be appropriate.)

a   Ask Y if its function is important enough that Y would be willing to not interrupt X so that it could receive the same treatment in return. Ask X if it was not interrupted by Y would it be willing to not interrupt Y?

4. Ask each part if it will actually agree to do the above for a specified amount of time. If either part becomes dissatisfied for any reason it is to signal the person that there is a need to renegotiate.

5) Ecological check: "Are there any other parts involved in this?" Are there any other parts that interrupt this part or that utilize these interruptions?" if so, renegotiate.

CREATING A PART, OUTLINE

1. Identify the desired outcome, the function of what part? I want a part that will achieve X.

2. Access any historical experience of doing X, or anything similar. Step inside each experience and access all aspects of doing X or parts of X. Go through each memory in all representational systems.

3. Create a detailed set of images of how you would behave if you were actually demonstrating whatever this part of you is going to have to do to achieve the outcome X.

4. First create a dissociated visual and auditory constructed movie.
   a. When you see a whole sequence that you're satisfied with, step inside the image and go through the whole sequence again from the inside, feeling what it is like to do these behaviors.

b.   If you are not satisfied, go back to 3A and change the movie. Do this until you are satisfied with that fantasy from the inside as well as from the outside.

5.   Ecological check. "Does any part object to my having a part which will be in charge of making that fantasy a reality?" Make sure you check in all representational systems to find all objecting parts. For each objecting part:
   a.   Ask that part to intensify the signal for "yes" and decrease for "no".
   b.   Ask "What is your function for me?" "What do you do for me?"
   c.   If the function doesn't tell you what the part's objection is ask, "What specifically is your objection or concerns".
   d.   Make a complete written list of all the parts that object and their functions.

6.   Satisfy all the objecting parts:
   a.   Redefine the part you are creating to take into account all the functions and concerns of the objecting parts.
   b.   Go back to step 3 and make a new modified fantasy that will satisfy the concerns of each part that objected.
   c.   Check with every part to make sure that each one is satisfied that this new representation of the new part's behavior will not interfere with its function.

7.   Ask your unconscious resources to analyze that fantasy and to pool this information to build a part and give entity. Get what you need to know from this fantasy to be able to build a part of you that can do this exquisitely and easily, and at every moment that it needs to be done.

8. Test the part to make sure it is there:
   a.   Go inside and ask.

b. Future pace repeatedly.
c. Behaviorally engage the part to find if it responds appropriately.

FAST PHOBIA CURE, MODIFIED

This procedure works usually in one session. It is most important to verify that the patient does have a phobia and if the phobia interferes with them trying to have a normal lifestyle. We must remember that fear is normal, even healthy at times. It is our internal warning system that we should listen to. The procedure is simple and normally only takes about thirty minutes.

1. Verify phobia, fight or flight.

2. Establish trance state and ideomotor signaling.

3. Establish a 3-place dissociation.
   a. Walk into the theater and look around.
   b. Have a seat in the middle of the theater.
   c. Float out of body, back to projection booth (look through window, stay in booth).

4. Run black & white movie.
   a. See still black & white picture of self prior to the phobic response.
   b. Turn still black & white picture into a movie. Play through phobic experience to point of safety afterwards and turn back into a still black & white picture.

5. Run movie backwards.
   a. Leave booth, walk past self-seated up to screen.
   b. Turn picture into color.
   c. Step into screen, experience.
   d. Play movie backwards "FAST" 2 seconds or less through the phobic experience to a point of the first still picture and stop. Do this at least three times.

6. Run the movie forward.
   a. Movie at normal speed.
   b. Observe client for phobic reaction.
   c. If phobic reaction returns, repeat the process.

You can start this procedure without inducing trance. As the client turns his thoughts inwards, he will enter into a trance-like state. This procedure can also be done after the formal introduction of trance and ideomoter signaling is established.

Hypnotic Approaches in Pain Management

Amnesia: Helps the patient forget about the pain via distraction.

a. Do not use the word "pain".
b. Do not remind the patient of the problem.
c. Explain to the patient how the disassociation works.

Anesthesia: To remove or make numb the pain in a given area.

a. Best not to remove 100% of the feelings. A patient may re-injure himself.
b. Need to keep some feelings or the patient will feel somewhat handicapped.

Analgesia: Similar to anesthesia, but pain is removed/reduced, but the tactile sensation and pressure is still there.

a. Use terms of analogies to remove pain.
b. "Melting slowly away like a small ice cube".

Symptom Substitution: Replace original feelings with a better feeling.

a. Describing pain as warm instead of cold.
b. Describe pain as comfortably cool instead of hot.
c. Working in direct opposition to the current feeling.

Teaching Disassociation: Teach the patient to disassociate from pain.

a. "Leave the pain here and move to the other side of the room".
b. "Taking your mind on a shopping trip to the mall".
c. Confuse the patient, move the pain to a healthy area of the body so the pain can be dealt with efficiently.

Fractional Approach: Talking about the patient losing a percentage of pain.

a. Start at 5%, then slowly move ahead in increments of 5% going to 90% of pain removal. Then telling the patient we should settle for 80% of pain removed.

Autohypnosis: Putting the patient in charge of their pain management.

a. Teach the patient how to go into trance by himself.
b. Assist the patient in developing his suggestions using the rules of self-hypnosis.

Headache Relief Without Trance: Having the patient visually disassociate from the headache.

a.　Have the patient assign a "color" to their headache.
b.　Ask them to turn that color a shade lighter.
c.　Continue going lighter, switching to other lighter colors as you go.
d.　Continue this procedure for 3 to 5 minutes.

Extra Thoughts

If the patient still appears reluctant or doubtful, start with establishing a "yes" set to illicit a positive framework.

Always be prepared to shift from one procedure to another if needed. It is very difficult to know in advance what will work best in that patient's model of the world.

SMOKING ABATEMENT SCRIPT

You are a very busy person, and so am I. You have lots of things to do now (name), before time comes to an end. Because there is so much to do, you must buy the extra time now. When one has much they want to do, and a way to do it (name), buy this time to do it all, at a very inexpensive price, it would be foolish, it's so comforting to know that there are people who care about and enjoy us. Different strokes for different folks is an old saying. Some people like red, and others like blue. Some people like vanilla, and some people hate it. Some people think that to be sociable they must do as their friends do. If your friends drank poison, could you see yourself being sociable by drinking it too? If your friends shot up with dangerous drugs, could you see yourself being sociable by shooting up too? If your friends jumped in front of a freight train, could you see yourself being sociable by jumping too? Is that the way to be sociable? If your friends inhaled killer poisonous fumes from the end of a little round tube, could you see yourself being sociable by inhaling those fumes too? Isn't it time to buy time by changing ideas: It's an easy price to pay for the time needed to do all one wants to do. And don't you think that relaxation and comfort are derived from talk and companionship and trying new experiences? And don't you think that true happiness is doing what is best for the self, regardless of what others are doing? Buying that extra time is easy and cheap. If one were drinking poison to be sociable, wouldn't one. To buy extra time quit now (name). And if one were shooting up with drugs to be sociable, wouldn't one, to buy extra time quit now. And since one was inhaling killer poisonous fumes from a little round tube, hasn't one, quit now. Good, because now one has easily bought and paid for that extra time, all that is needed and wanted to do the lots there are to do. Now one can walk again, now one can breathe again, and one can enjoy the relaxing comfort of a healthy life, just because of a change of ideas now (name). One can feel relaxed while walking and feel relaxed while talking and feel at ease while socializing without poison, even if our friends are poisoning themselves. Because we've begun to care about ourselves. Because we are # 1, and we matter most and extra time was bought so easily now (Terminate).

Stop Smoking, Reframed

This is one of the longest stop smoking interventions available. While longer it usually produces better results. It is also important to have your patient surrender their cigarettes and matches before beginning the intervention. You must also bear in mind that you need to work within the patient's model of the world.

1. Interview with the client: Assess the client's motivation for wanting to stop smoking. Does the client want to stop smoking because of the influence of others, or for himself? Have the client clearly establish what the positive and negative influences surrounding his smoking of cigarettes are (Have client surrender their cigarettes and lighter to you, no exceptions!).

2. Induce trance using a suitable technique, induce trance and deepen to the state of somnambulism. Now take the client through the six step refraining process. Once completed, future pace the client and have

them see themselves as a nonsmoker. Spend at least five minutes on this, having the client see himself as a non-smoker in cigarette smoking situations, and ask him how they will handle the situations.

3. Bring the client up from trance. Ask the client to share how he felt about the total experience. If possible, have the client return for two more sessions in the next four days. This will allow you to reinforce this technique or utilize a different one.

Another thought on stop smoking interventions is to employ the use of a grieving situation in trance. This would allow the patient to say goodbye to his old friend, cigarettes. For many patients their cigarettes have been with them through the good times and the bad times, even when others have failed them, the cigarettes have been there for them. I would urge you to consider this idea for the chronic cigarette smoker.

Smoking Abstinence Script

Now many people have come to me and ask for help in solving some particular difficulty, and they say to me, "I have no motivation, I have no discipline", and I say to them, "The unmotivated person doesn't call for an appointment. The undisciplined person doesn't show up on time". The unmotivated person does not distinguish the place they wish to be, from the place where they are now. The undisciplined person stays home. Now you have all the motivation you need, you have all the discipline you need though there is one thing you still need which you don't have yet, and that's self-confidence. The self-confidence it takes to set out on a journey completely prepared for the trip, knowing you've read the map, you've charted the course, reservations taken care of, believing you can, will, reach your destination quickly, easily, effortlessly. The self-confidence it takes to recognize all the signs of success. Just as now, you recognize those comfortable hypnotic sensations in the hands, arms, legs, those physical signs that allow you to know you've traveled from one state to another state in a calm and confident way, and you can offer yourself large portions of self-confidence, large portions of self-esteem. You can breathe in self-confidence and breathe out self-doubt as you continue to enjoy the journey toward your goal. Throughout the years that I have worked with people I have had many clients come here with a very interesting problem. They have become obsessed with the idea of making love with someone they are attracted to, and when they have raised the subject with the object of their desire they've been told, in no uncertain terms, that a physical relationship was impossibile, and the reasons given for the impossibility have been many. It is to dangerous or risky, unhealthy or even unethical, and yet, faced with all these obstacles, these clients become more and more obsessed, convinced that their happiness depends on the consummation of their desires, to the neglect of all other aspects of their lives. Which reminds me of the man who had just bought a brand new house, an expensive house in the nicest part of town. He had admired that house for many, many years, maybe since he was a teenager, maybe from his twenties, he couldn't remember exactly but he did know he'd been wanting to buy that house for a long, long time, and now here it was. All his, he lavished care and attention on it, decorated it in tasteful colors of (insert color of client's clothing). He papered and painted and hardly paid any attention at all to that growing headache at first, in fact it was several years before he noticed that his head seemed to have a continuous dull ache, and his muscles were aching as well. He felt tired a lot too. So he visited a doctor who gave him a prescription but he just never felt much better and everything failed to stop that headache, or the irritation and the insidious feeling that his health was fading away, but at least he had his house, and it is easy to understand how he might feel if you've ever gone from house to house. Real estate open houses perhaps, or just going to someone else's home, seeing how the other half lives can be an educational experience, but I can understand my client's obsession with something that's not about to happen, from the day I saw my dream house. Of course the price was very beyond what I could possibly afford, and yet I couldn't get it out of my mind. I imagined myself in the living room, in the den, and was certain I must have it to be happy. Now everybody knows that nobody likes to be told what to do, and if I could tell you what to do you wouldn't have to be here today. You'd call me on the phone, you'd say," I'd like to quit smoking", and I would say, "That's a wonderful idea, quit smoking, now?" But everybody knows nobody likes to be told what to do, so I won't say to you, you already know all the reasons for ending this smoking problem. I wouldn't have to say to you that smoking is dangerous and unhealthy. I wouldn't have to tell you that you would receive no pleasure from smoking. I never need to say that cigarettes are a poor substitute for (insert client's rational for smoking) But one thing I will say to you is; "Not smoking is not a task you wouldn't find easy" when you leave here today you'll no longer be somebody who smokes, You know you have the desire to smoke, and you know you know it, and no one can talk you out of it, but what you know now that you didn't know before, is you also have a large amount of no desire, and you can get to know this place of no desire as it expands and grows larger and larger, and the feeling of no desire can reach deeper and deeper, the time of now desire continues to lengthen, and no way is easier than this, and I read once, when I was a child, I thought like a child, I acted like a child. Now that I am grown I put away the things of childhood, what does that really mean? I'm not sure, but it certainly meant a lot to clients who were obsessed with a sexual desire that could never be fulfilled. Perhaps it was the thought of putting old ways behind them that finally allowed them to be free, or perhaps they simply grew up and took responsibility for their feelings and their behavior. Disappointment is something we all face from time to time, and you can imagine how disappointed that man was to learn there was insecticide in the floor and walls of that house. He went on his dream vacation, and was amazed to discover his headaches and sickness disappeared in just a few days time. When he got home he contacted an expert in the field. The expert gently broke the news, his entire house was slowly being poisoned and so was he. It only took him one day to pack his things. He knew for certain his health was worth more than any house. No matter how long he'd wanted it, and I guess I finally came to terms with the fact that I couldn't buy a $300,000 home, no matter what I did. It was a nice dream, but the price was to high to pay, especially since there was no Jacuzzi and it is good to finally resolve those feelings and to just let go, not needing to now how the unconscious mind knows what to do for you, thinking with an awareness of things thought, without needing to know those things which will get done automatically, you know what to do. Now I'd prefer you stop smoking immediately, but it's entirely up to you to discover today the best time and way for you. Some clients wait an hour, some wait until after dinner, some stop entirely right before bed. Now, I'd prefer you stop immediately, but it's completely up to you to choose the time, a time today, when you free yourself from smoking, forever.

Adults With Abusive Childhood Issues

Application: For those patients still bothered by childhood abuse issues, physical, emotional and sexual.

Move the patient down in trance to a medium state, read the following script slowly as you continue to pace the patient's breathing throughout trance.

You know, and I know, that nothing can undo what happened to you in the past, what was done to you back then, but that was then, and this is now, you can stop the pain and fear, you can put an end to it, now, and you already know how, you know how to forget to pay attention to particular things, you know how to shut doors and windows on the past, you know how to see things now for what they are now, not what was, and your unconscious knows how to walk forward in time across that line, a boundary line that marks a new beginning, that lets you join the present, as you let go of the past, that lets you see a future, when you will remember how good it felt today to let go of that past, to say good-bye to it, and to let yourself feel okay so go ahead now and keep going ahead later on, because that past is through and you are just you here and now, and when you get home, there is something you can do to put this away and get on with the future, some way for you, a ritual per-haps, a ceremonial letting go, throwing something away to let yourself know that the past is done and the future has begun, and you will do that, will you not?

ANXIETY SCRIPT

It is recommended to use this metaphor for clients with panic attacks and general anxiety.

Take the client to at least a medium state of trance and tell this story as you continue to pace his breathing.

It has been suggested, by a French physician, that when babies are born, they should not be held upside down in a cold, bright noisy operating room, and spanked to make them cry, instead they should be born into a warm, quiet room with soft, gentle lights and put into a warm bath, because when they are treated that way, they open their eyes and look around, they seem amazed and happy. They even seem to smile, they lie there quietly relaxed, and they grow up to be happier and more secure, all because they were treated gently, protected and taken care of, not hurt or scared, but just allowed to be safe and quiet for a while, a natural way of doing things that seems to work out well, because almost all animals have their babies on warm spring nights when it is safe to be born, and the mother can take care of them, and help them get used to things, slowly and comfortably adjust to things, and learn how to keep things under control They learn to hide quietly in the tall grass, how to remain very still, even when there is danger near, and they learn to play happily, secure in the awareness that someone is nearby, protecting them, calmly watching out for them, and as they get older and wiser, they seem to calm down themselves, and become more quiet inside and out, as they use everything they've learned, because even a brief moment can provide a lesson to be used to keep oneself calm and quiet inside, the way warm water can seep throughout, even though only a small corner rests gently in that warm bath where a new born child rests and smiles, with a warm glow of safe comfort.

Escalator Technique

The technique used in this script is excellent for being able to go deep into self-hypnosis. This would also be a good script to put on a cassette tape for your use. Practice is the key to your success with any of these self-hypnotic techniques listed in this book.

Take a comfortable position in your chair. Close your eyes and breathe deeply two or three times. Now that you are comfortable, you will listen closely to my voice and follow all the suggestions given. Your eyes are now closed, take another deep breath, hold it a few seconds, and let it out. Mentally say to yourself, relax deeply, relax deeply, the more you can relax, and the more you concentrate, the deeper you will go into hypnosis. Let all your muscles go as loose and limp as possible. To do this, start with your right leg, tighten the muscles first, make the leg rigid, and then let it relax from your toe right up to your hip. Then tighten the muscles of the left leg, let that leg relax from the toes up. Let the stomach and abdominal area relax, then your chest and breathing muscles. The muscles of your back can loosen, your shoulders and neck muscles relaxing. Often we have tension in these areas. Let all these muscles relax. Now your arms right down to your finger tips. Even your facial muscles will relax; relaxation is so pleasant and comfortable. Let go completely and enjoy the relaxation. All tension seems to drain away and you soon find a listlessness creeping over you, with a sense of comfort and well being. As you relax more and more, you will slip deeper and deeper into hypnosis. Your arms and legs may develop a feeling of heaviness, or instead you find your whole body feeling very light, as though you are floating on a soft cloud. Allow yourself to experience any such sensation you are having for a minute. Just let yourself go and feel the sensation of floating, or heaviness, or any other sensation you are experiencing. Now listen to me and imagine that you are standing at the top of an escalator such as those found in stores. See the steps moving down in front of you, and you see the railings. I am going to count from ten to zero, as I start to count imagine that you are stepping on the escalator, standing there with your hands on the railing while the steps move down in front of you, taking you with them, if you prefer, you can imagine a staircase or an elevator instead. If you have any difficulty visualizing the escalator or staircase or elevator just the count its self will take you deeper and deeper (Slowly). Ten, now you step on and start going down, nine…eight…seven…six, going deeper and deeper with each count. Five…four…three, still deeper. Two…one…and zero. Now you step off at the bottom and you will continue to go deeper still with each breath you take, deeper and deeper with each breath. You are so relaxed and so comfortable. Let go still more, notice your breathing, probably it is now slower and you are breathing more from the bottom of your lungs, abdominal breathing, as you go deeper into hypnosis, my voice may seem to drift away from you as though it were coming from a great distance, but you shall continue to hear it and pay attention to the suggestions I shall make to you. You will be able to respond to these suggestions even though you are very relaxed and very comfortable. Now you can imagine yourself to be strolling down the hall to a special room…a special room in your own mind…as you see yourself strolling down the hall, feeling fine, feeling pleasant and relaxed, you can indicate to yourself when you reach the room, you can have it any way you wish it to be. It can be large or small, light or dark, cool or warm, furnished in any way you wish so that it is pleasant, comfortable and attractive. Now, approaching the door to this special room, now seeing yourself opening the door, entering the room, and closing the door. You can arrange yourself in any position that is comfortable, sitting, lying down, or strolling about. As you see yourself in this situation, you can allow yourself to go deeper and deeper, into a very deep state of concentration, a very deep state of relaxation. You know that you can always return to this special room in your mind when you wish to do so. You will be able to learn to use these techniques and these procedures for your own benefit and your own welfare, so that you can learn to relax and rest more deeply, study and concentrate more deeply, and to gain more self understanding and more self control. As you continue to use self-hypnosis, you are going to gain more self confidence in your ability to accomplish your purposes. You will find that you are able to follow the suggestions you make to yourself in the trance state. You will find yourself able to go quickly into the trance state whenever you wish to do so, to go into hypnosis, all you have to do is close your eyes, make yourself comfortable, and drift into hypnosis. Some times it may help to think to yourself the phrase, " Now I am going into hypnosis", and repeat to yourself the words, "relax deeply, relax deeply, relax deeply," saying them very slowly. As you do this you will slip off into hypnosis. You say nothing aloud, you merely think these words. When you have do this take another deep breath to help you relax more and go through the relaxation just as you have done before. Tell your muscles to relax, as I have done. When you have finally relaxed your arms, imagine the escalator, elevator or staircase. Now you should count backwards from ten to zero, including the zero, count slowly. When ever you are ready to awaken all you need to do is think to yourself, "Now I am going to wake up". Then count slowly to five and you will be wide awake. You will always awaken refreshed, relaxed and feeling fine. While you are in hypnosis, if something should happen so that you awaken, you do so instantly and spontaneously. Something such as a phone ringing or a real emergency like a fire you will awaken instantly and be wide awake and fully alert. Actually this would happen without such a suggestion being necessary, because your subconscious mind always protects you. Now you are resting comfortably, and you are in a hypnotic trance. Now let yourself experience deeper and deeper into the trance. Just pay attention to your breathing, notice how deep and regular your breathing is, you can go deeper into hypnosis with each breath you take, let each breath carry you deeper and deeper and deeper. Just like going to sleep except that you will keep hearing my voice and following my instructions. Now, continue to go deeper into hypnosis, to become more and more comfortable with each breath that you take. Breathing rhythmically and deeply, going deeper with each breath, let yourself go completely now, deeper and deeper, now that you are deeply relaxed, I want you to remain that way for a few minutes while you have an interesting and pleasant experience. I will not tell you what to experience, you can have the kind of experience that you choose to have, it may be a surprise to you, it may be a feeling or a memory, or a thought, you just let yourself experience it and enjoy it. As you have this experience you can go deeper and deeper into hypnosis. Now take a few minutes to let yourself experience whatever happens (three to four minute pause). In a few moments you will be able to complete the thought, feeling or memory. Now imagine that you are standing at the top of an escalator again. See the steps moving down in front of you, and see the railings. I am going to count from ten to zero, as I start to count, imagine that you are stepping on to the escalator, standing there with your hands on the railings while the steps move down in front of you, taking you with them. Ten…now you step on and start going down, nine …eight…seven…six…, going deeper and deeper with each count, five…four…three…still deeper, two…one…and zero. Now you step off at the bottom and will continue to go deeper and deeper with each breath you take, deeper and deeper with each breath, you are so relaxed and so comfortable. Let go still more. Now I want you to make a suggestion to yourself that you want to carry out. You can stay in a trance while you decide what suggestion you want to make, deciding will be easy, and it also will be easy for you to follow the suggestion whenever you wish to complete it. Go ahead now, and make your suggestion. Take whatever time you need, and after you have made your suggestion, you may arouse yourself from the trance at any time you wish and be wide awake and alert. You will be able to practice these techniques whenever you wish to do so, and you can learn to use them for your own benefit and your own welfare, so that you can become the kind of person you wish to be…the kind of person you can be.

Balloon Technique

This technique can be used for intervention with various problems, i.e., grieving, stop smoking and habit control.

During the assessment interview note the significant points that stops a person from achieving the desired change.

Take the patient into trance and deepen to somnambulism.

Ask the patient to go to his special place, a place that he feels comfortable, safe and secure. Build the intensity of his special place.

Sample script/example for stop smoking and the significant points to overcome are for an example;

(1) Craving tobacco (2) Light headiness (3) Unspecified anxiety.

Enjoying your special place, knowing that you are comfortable and safe there, Notice the colors about your special place, how very nice, notice all the other things about your special place, the sights, the sounds, the colors, no one else can be in your special place unless you allow them, what a wonderful place to be, so comfortable and safe in your special place, so wonderful, notice how you feel, comfortable and safe, enjoying your special place. Notice that in your (left) (right) hand you are holding three balloons, three of the ugliest balloons you have ever seen in your life, these ugly balloons look so out of place in your special place, these are such ugly repulsive colors on these balloons, the first balloon has the words, "craving tobacco" written on the side, the words are clear and easy to read, the second ugly balloon has the words "light headiness" clearly printed on the side, the third ugly balloon has the word "anxiety" clearly on the side, there you stand with these three very ugly balloons with the words, "craving tobacco", "light headiness" and "anxiety" written on the balloons, ugly balloons certainly do not belong in your special place. As you observe these ugly balloons with the words on them, you realize even more that they don't belong in your special, beautiful place, When you are ready you can release these ugly balloons and watch them slowly float up and away, moving slowly out of sight. As the balloons start to fade away, so do the words printed on them, remembering briefly that the words were "craving tobacco", "light headiness" and "anxiety". Watch them slowly disappear from sight (Pause). Now you can see yourself in your special place, free of the ugly balloons, free of the tobacco craving, light headiness and anxiety, seeing yourself in your special place as a nonsmoker, noticing how you look now, how wonderful, notice how very wonderful you feel, feeling so proud of yourself now that you are a nonsmoker, how wonderful to be so rightfully proud of yourself, seeing yourself as a nonsmoker, experiencing how it feels to be a nonsmoker, how wonderful. Continue to relax, perhaps moving even one level deeper, enjoying the experience of being a nonsmoker. Bring client out of trance and process the experience.

Migraine Headache Intervention

Initiate this script after taking patient into a least at medium state and continue to pace their breathing throughout the trance experience.

Now while you relax and allow yourself to experience the variety of changes as you drift into a trance, I would like to help you to learn how to change those things that allow you to be able to prevent or reduce your headaches, and the thing you need to do that when you feel a headache coming on, what you need to do is be able to allow your hands, and feet to become very warm or hot very quickly, so as you pay attention to those hands and feet, I would like you to realize that you can imagine how it feels to have those hands and feet sitting in the hot rays of the sun ...or resting in the warm water of a bath...or whatever other image comes to mind when you begin to pay attention to that warmth there...and begin to feel the warmth grow, getting warmer and warmer, almost hot, comfortably swollen and warm, a warmth that may seem to spread into the arms and legs after a time, and as that warmth grows and becomes more clear in your awareness, you can continue to relax and drift down into a comfortable trance state, where your unconscious mind can find it's own way to let your mind become aware of that warmth and heaviness, a growing warmth and relaxation in the fingers of that hand, and the other hand, and the feet in your shoes, and your arms and legs too, perhaps, heavy and warm, warm and heavy, that's right, and from now on when-ever you feel a headache coming on, what you need to do, and can do, is to relax in this way, remembering the quiet heaviness, and allow that warm thought to return, greater than before perhaps, until you feel that warmth everywhere, or just in those hands and feet, because now you can buy gloves and socks that heat up by themselves, powered by little batter-ies that make those thick gloves warm, and make those soft socks hot, almost as soon as you put them on, they begin to get warmer and warmer, you can try them on in a store and actually feel that heat increase, as they give off their own heat, a surprising feeling of warmth that works so well, they use them in Alaska where even the bitter cold is soon replaced by the pulsating warmth, as those gloves heat up, and those socks heat up, and the hands and feet begin to thaw, begin to feel soft, swollen and warm, swollen with a comfortable feeling that spreads up the arms, and it continues on with you even after you drift upwards to a wakeful awareness, and reach that point where the eyes open, that's right, drifting upwards now, as that warm feeling continues, a nice warm feel-ing that you can create anytime you need to, anytime you want to, that's right, a warm wakefulness now, as the mind drifts up and the eyes are allowed to open......(Terminate trance)

MEETING THE INNER CHILD

The purpose of this exercise is to assist the patient in getting in touch with his inner child. This in itself should generate insight for the patient as to what his present needs might be, and lend additional insight into lifelong behaviors.

Take client down in trance, medium state. Tell the client the following story, pacing his breathing throughout trance.

Think back now to when you were 7 or 8 years old (pause). Now picture in your mind the place you lived when you were that age (pause). Now imagine that you are standing outside that very place looking at it, now walk around to the door you mainly used when you were a child, slowly now open the door and walk in, notice the sights, sounds and smells that were familiar to you (pause). Continue to walk to the room where you used to feel the most secure and comfortable in. As that 7 or 8 year old child, notice what you are doing, how were you dressed? (pause) Now tell the child the most important and valuable information that he or she can use in his coming years now that you are an adult and have lived those years (pause). Go ahead now and speak to the child and tell him what he needs to know (pause). Now give the child a hug before you leave, if you can't hug the child, and then just say good-bye (Pause). Now turn and walk back out the same way you came in. Continue to walk to the location where you first viewed the place where you lived (Terminate trance, ensuring that you empower the client's memory).

You can expect this experience to be very strong and profound for some clients. You need to ask your clients to explain their experience in detail to you.

THE JOURNEY OF LEARNING

This intervention allows the patient to look into their mind's eye to the future so they may decide for themselves what behavioral changes they wish to address.

Picture yourself walking slowly down the mountain, becoming more relaxed with each step you take. Each breeze that caresses your body relaxes you more and more. The path is made up of switchbacks and each time you change direction you'll double your relaxation (pause). You're about a third of the way down the mountain, enjoying every step, feeling a comfortable breeze blowing, keeping you not too hot and not too cool, but just right. You stop and look up at the clouds against a beautiful blue sky. Take a deep breath now, and peacefulness overtakes you and you continue down, deeper down the mountain. You've become more relaxed with each step that is taken. Allowing every muscle in your face, neck and shoulders to let go of any tension. Your legs and feet feel great, walking down the mountain brings pleasure to your heart and body (pause). You are half way down the mountain, you see a place to stop and take a break. There is a tree and a stream and you are able to watch the birds fly about, taking some time to relax yourself deeper, deeper relaxed than you've been before (pause). Its now time to journey to the bottom of the mountain and relax much more deeply now, down, down slowly deeper down the mountain in complete joy, peace, strength and energy. Nothing bothers you, nothing disturbs you in any way the peace that passes all understanding is yours. Feelings of love and acceptance of who you are, are yours. As you reach the bottom of the mountain you notice a fork in the path. You must make a decision which path to take. If you go to the left, you will experience your future with no changes. If you choose to go to the right, you can experience the changes you want to make now. First let us experience the left path, keeping all your behaviors, beliefs, and attitudes, see what your life is like for you now. What is it costing you physically, emotionally spiritually and financially? (Short pause) how do you feel? What do you say to yourself? (8-second pause) Now go 5 years into the future. Look at yourself in the mirror; are you happy with what you see? (Short pause) What are your behaviors costing you? Financially, emotionally, socially and spiritually? (5-second pause) How do you feel about yourself? (Pause) What are you saying to yourself while you look into the mirror? (Pause) Now lets go ten years into the future. Look at yourself in the mirror; are you happy with what you see? (Pause) What are your behaviors costing you? Financially, emotionally, socially and spiritually? (Pause) How do you feel about yourself? (Pause) What are you saying to yourself while you look into the mirror? (Pause) Now I want you to go to the time when you're rocking in a rocking chair and reflecting on your whole life, what do you say to yourself? (Pause) What do you wish you had done differently? (Pause) What behaviors do you wish you had changed? What attitudes have hindered you? What beliefs about you and others have limited you? Is this the life you wanted? What learning can aid you back in the present? (Pause) Come back now to the crossroads and let's travel the path to the right. Take a couple of nice deep breaths, letting go. Now in your mind's eye experience yourself making the changes that are important to you (pause). Who you are tomorrow depends on the decisions you make today. Behaviors you want to change, beliefs about yourself that are limiting you. What new beliefs could you now believe about yourself and others? (pause) What new attitudes can enhance your life? (Pause) Now let's journey one year into your future, look in the mirror. See some of the positive changes that have taken place. How do you feel? (pause) What do you say to yourself? (pause) How have these changes affected you emotionally, socially, physically and financially? (pause) What other areas in your life are different? (pause) Now go five years into the future, look at yourself in the mirror, how happy are you with the changes you've made? (pause) How have the changes affected you? (pause) look into that mirror, what do you say to yourself? (Pause) Now go ten years into the future, look at yourself in the mirror, how happy are you with the changes you've made? (pause) How have the changes affected you? (Pause) Look into the mirror, what do you say to yourself? (pause) Now go twenty years into the future, look at yourself in the mirror, how happy are you with the changes you've made? (pause) How have the changes affected you? (Pause) Look in to the mirror, what do you say to yourself? (pause) Now go fifty years into the future, look at yourself in the mirror, how happy are you now with the changes you have made? (pause) How have these changes affected you? (pause) Look into the mirror again, what do you say to yourself? (Pause) Now I want you to go to the time when you are rocking in a rocking chair, reflecting on your whole life. See how making one or two changes can make a difference on the outcome of your life. A change in a behavior, belief or attitude can have a rippling effect in many ways and in many areas of your life. How is your life richer financially? (Pause) How is your life richer spiritually? (pause) What have been the benefits in terms of significant others, family, friends and others? (pause) What other areas of your life have you improved? (pause) Now what are you saying to yourself? (pause) How do you feel about yourself knowing changes have taken place? (pause) What is it like to look in the mirror at yourself? Enjoy it, intensify it! Come back to the present, today, and know that all of it is yours, the choices are yours. (Terminate trance)

ULCER SCRIPT

This is a good intervention for your patients that suffer from ulcers. The problem of ulcers is fairly common with middle and late stage alcoholics. Use this in trance when the patient is deepened to a medium state, always pacing the breathing during trance.

Everyone is familiar with Smokey the Bear, and his pleas with campers to make sure their fires are completely out, so every scout learns how to put fires out, to make sure everything is cool, nothing left smoldering or hot, by pouring water on it, or dumping snow on it, just the way you're suppose to, keeping it cool while relaxing in the shade and drinking a tall glass of ice water and watching that coolness spread, making sure it's completely out so you can leave the woods feeling relaxed and calm knowing nothing will catch and spread, because fire is to hot to handle unless you wear special gloves, insulated and made of fireproof materials which used to be very thick and heavy, but now there is a new material coated with a very

thin layer of metal which is shiny and reflects all the heat, and keeps everything cool, even down to absolute zero, which is as cold as things can get,
but they cool off nuclear reactors in a very different way, because when a
reactor gets hot it means there are to many electrons flying around inside,
so they lower in carbon rods that absorbs those electrons, absorbs all that
energy, and as things quiet down, they also cool off, like turning off a
spigot to quiet that dripping sound, shutting off the valve that stops the
flow in there, they can also coat the walls with something cool and thick,
like they do in houses, to insulate and protect, to keep the people inside
comfortable in any weather, the way skin protects us from many things,
but when it gets cut or scratched it needs to grow back together to heal
that tiny hole, and so we take care of it, put a bandaid over it, and are care-
ful not to bump it, not to irritate it, because it's okay to irritate things, to
keep them cool and wet, but we try not to irritate things, especially not
wild animals that live in forests and parks, the places we're suppose to protect by putting those fires out, the way rangers do, always looking out for
smoke and rushing to put it out, before it gets out of control, which you
can do too, wherever you go, wherever you are, even asleep at night, when
those alarms begin to sound, putting it out without a thought, and returning to a deep, restful sleep, secure in this awareness, that you can take care
of you. (Terminate trance)

RAISING SELF-ESTEEM

This is a long-standing problem for the chemically dependent in early recovery. Take the patient to at least a medium state of trance and read the following script while pacing their breathing. Reinforce in future sessions as needed.

Do you know of Beethoven who became increasingly deaf as he got older, but kept on working, writing music that he could not hear, until one day, one evening, he conducted the symphony as they played his newest work, a concerto, and when it was finished the crowd erupted in applause, they stood and cheered, but he could not hear, he stood there facing the orchestra, unaware of the audience's approval until someone walked out and turned him around so he could see what he could not hear, only then did he know what everyone needs to know, but sometimes can't hear, like the woman I have heard of, black hair, black eyes, stocky build, a bright professional woman who hated herself and hated her life, she thought she was

ugly and awful, and she thought that was why so many awful things had happened to her, but one day she was having lunch with a friend, an artist she had known for a time, and she said to her friend, that there were so many beautiful women, and they all seemed to be on that street that day, and her friend simply said, I think you're the most beautiful woman I've ever seen, and went on eating, as if it were nothing, and that simple observation, that simply statement of opinion, matter of fact, not flattery, wouldn't go away, couldn't be undone, her friend was an artist who knew what beauty was, so she could not ignore it, and she could not forget it, instead she begin to look at herself, each day in the mirror, and she began to look at others, how they looked, who they were with, and it was very hard and scary at first to realize how wrong she had been, how wrong her mother had been, how wrong she had been about herself in so many different ways, but over time she had began to accept it, she was not ugly, she was not stupid, she was not a bad person, she was attractive and likeable and nice, and she did not have to settle for less than she deserved, how she thought changed, how she felt changed, what she did changed, her life changed, all because of one brief comment, one brief glimpse of herself, a clear admission of something she had been unable to let herself know before, that truth is beauty and beauty truth, and the truth about oneself, one's beauty, is in the eye of the beholder, but what we hear is not always measured on a hearing test, Beethoven heard things in his mind that his ears could no longer hear, and many animals can hear sounds, that the human ear cannot, and all we ever need to hear is that there is nothing else we need to do, except hear the beauty of what is.
(Terminate trance)

Transient Pain Management

Applications: Dental work, surgery, sports injuries, sprains, headaches, child birthing,

Induce trance and read script pacing client's breathing pattern throughout the trance work.

You are sitting there comfortably aware that you have come here today because you want to gain control of your own abilities, to eliminate some future feelings of discomfort, and as you continue to relax and to drift down into a deep trance, I want you to take your time, not too fast, not too slow, because there are some things you need to listen to carefully, first you need to understand that you already have the ability to lose an arm or a hand, to become completely unaware of exactly where that arm is positioned, or what it is doing, and you have the ability to be not concerned about exactly where that arm is, or that hand or leg, or your entire body for that fact, this may seem to take too much effort to pay attention to at times, because you also have an unconscious ability you can learn how to use effectively, and that ability is to turn off the feeling in an arm, a leg, or anywhere you choose, and once you discover how it feels to not feel anything at all, wherever you want that to occur, then you can create the numb, comfortable feeling, anywhere, anytime it is useful to you, and I don't know whether your unconscious mind will allow you to discover that numb feeling in the right hand, or a finger of the left hand first, a tiny area of numbness, a comfortable tingling feeling, a heavy thick numbness, that seems to grow and spreads over time, until it covers that hand, the back of the hand, or anything else you pay close attention to, it's your choice, it just seems to disappear from your experience, but you don't know how it feels, to not feel something that isn't there, so here is what I want you to do, I want you to reach over to that numb area, to that numb hand, that's right, go ahead and touch it, (pause), and feel that touching as you begin to pinch yourself there, at first you may experience a feeling, but as you continue to pinch yourself, an interesting thing happens…(Slight pause) you begin to discover that there are times, when you feel nothing at all there, that's right, the feeling just seems to disappear, as you continue to learn how to allow your unconscious mind to turn off those feelings, all you need to do is just pay very close attention to the numbness, and as that ability grows and develops, and you begin to know, really know beyond a doubt, that you already do know how to allow feeling and pain to disappear from your hand, or anywhere, your other hand can return to a resting place of its choice, and you can drift up to that point where wakeful awareness will return, so go ahead now, as you relax, an discover how to let go and to feel that numbness more and more clearly, and you can drift up more, in your own time, in your own comfortable way, that's right, take your time to learn, and then drifting back upwards, eyes opening (pause) now, before you wake up completely, I would like you to close your eyes again, and allow that drifting down again, reentering that place of calm relaxation, perhaps going even deeper than before, while you drift down again, there is a story I want to tell you about a young boy on TV not long ago in the past, he had learned to control all of his pain, he described the steps he went down in his mind, one at a time down those steps, until he found this hall at the bottom, like a long tunnel, and all along the tunnel on both sides were many different switches, switchboxes, each clearly labeled, one for the right hand, one for the left, one for the leg, and one for every place on the body, and he could see the wires to those switches clearly, the nerves that carried the feelings from one place to another, all going through those switches and switchboxes, all he needed to do was to reach up in his mind and turn off the switches he wanted to, and then he could feel nothing at all, no feelings could get through from there, no feelings at all, because he had turned off those switches, he used his mind's abilities differently from the man who simply made his body numb, he didn't know how he did it exactly, all he knew was he relaxed and disconnected, like a train car disconnecting from the rest, moved his mind away from his body, moving it outside some place else, where he could watch and listen, but drift off some place else, and it really doesn't matter exactly how you tell your unconscious what to do, or how your unconscious does it for you, the only thing of importance is that you know you can lose the feelings as easily as closing your eyes, and drifting down within, where something unknown in the unconscious happens that allows you to disconnect from the uncomfortable feeling, that allows that numbness to occur …and then a drifting upwards now, upward towards the surface and slowly allowing the eyes to open as wakeful awareness returns.

If possible, before the client leaves your office, ask the client to practice making a body part numb. Ask the client to practice this as much as reasonably possible before the next session. Future sessions may, or may not require repeating this session.

CHRONIC PAIN MANAGEMENT

Applications: Long term pain, back injuries, nerve damage, phantom limb pain, and cancer.

Induce trance, read script pacing the patient's breathing pattern.

With your eyes closed, as you begin to relax, you probably notice that the first thing you notice is how difficult it is to not become aware of that pain and discomfort, and that's fine, you don't need to fight your mind which is always aware of those sensations there for you, because as you relax, you can begin to discover that each time you relax a muscle in your arm...or a leg...or your face...or even a foot...or a finger, that you can drift down more and more deeply than before, into that sensation there in a more relaxed and comfortable way, because there really is no need to make the effort it takes to try to stay away from that feeling or to try to fight that feeling, which almost seems to guide and direct awareness down toward it, more and more into it, and as you drift toward it, toward that center of that feeling, everything else can be allowed to relax, to relax more and more, as you begin to discover that it really is okay to let go in that way, to allow yourself to relax every other part of your body and to drift down toward the very tiniest center of that feeling, the very small middle of it, the source of it, and then to drift down through that center into a place beneath it of quietness and calm awareness, down through that feeling, and out the other side, into a space of relaxed letting go, of comfortable relaxation, where the mind can drift, the way waves drift from one place to another as that body relaxes and the mind becomes smoother and smoother, able to absorb events, even those events, easily and comfortably, to become absorbed in thoughts and images, as the mind reflects the clear wonder of a child, a young child, watching a flock of geese as they soar across the sky and fly into the mist, the rhythm of their sound becoming softer and softer, as soft as the down in a pillow in a place where you rest and relax, a most comfortable place for a child to relax and drift into dreams through the mind, protected and safe, where the letting go allows the flow and the soft floating upwards, where the mind drifts free of things far below, and seems to soar in a sky as clear as glass, so smooth and clear that it disappears when you look into it, and what appears instead is the deep blue shine of the warm soft sun, a star far beyond that reaches out and provides that warm soft light as you drift down and experience the comfort and learn to feel the sound sleep that your unconscious mind can provide you whenever you relax and allow it to drift into a trance, because it can take you down through that feeling, into a space, that relaxed comfortable place, as you relax and allow it to do so just for you, that relief and relaxation, that drifting down through which comes to you whenever you allow it to, just as that drifting upwards occurs as well, a drifting back toward the surface of wakeful awareness, as your unconscious mind reminds you to drift up in a relaxed, comfortable way, back towards the surface now, bring with you that comfortable relaxation, that automatic change in sensation, even as the mind drifts upwards, the relaxation continues, as the mind awakens and the eyes open, but the body remains behind, relaxed, that's right, eyes open now (pause) but before you come back completely, you can close those eyes again, and feel that relaxation again, and recognize that ability, that ability to relax, to let your unconscious mind find the way to provide you with more and more comfort, more and more relaxed, letting go, that's right, aware that you can do so, anytime, anyplace you need or want to, you can return to that place, so here is what you do, later on today, tomorrow, next week, and for the rest of your life, whenever you need to or want to, you can close your eyes just for a moment, perhaps, and feel that comfortable feeling, that change in sensation return to you, and you drift into that light trance, or a deep trance, where your unconscious mind can take care of you, make things comfortable for you, and then you return to the surface of wakeful awareness, not needing to make the effort it takes to try to tell if that feeling is there or not, just as you return now back to the surface, comfortably relaxed and refreshed, remaining relaxed perhaps.

Improved Study Habits

This intervention is especially good for high school and college students that feel the need to improve their study habits. Start this procedure at somnambulism.

You are going to experience a completely successful study period, a completely successful study period; you will (for example) study at a table near the window on the third floor of the library. Now just imagine yourself comfortable as you prepare to study you arrange your materials, your papers, your books in front of you, you take a deep breath, exhale and relax, take another deep breath, pause, exhale and relax, and you begin to focus on the work in front of you. You will begin at (insert time) and you will stop at (insert time). Within this block of time, you will focus completely on the work at hand because you are enthusiastic and eager to absorb all the information that you need. You concentrate completely, all the normal sounds around you fade out as you find yourself absorbed in your studies. You feel calm, relaxed, and nothing disturbs your concentration and you work at your peak, absorbing and retaining all the information you need. When the time is up a signal from your subconscious will alert you, tell you that you have completed your work and you take a deep breath and you are relaxed and have plenty of energy for other activities. Repeat this procedure as needed, three times would be recommended for maximum effectiveness.

Stress Reduction Intervention

No doubt you will have numerous patients that this intervention will apply to, as stress is a high profile problem in our society. Start this script when you have deepened the patient to the medium state.

Because you are now relaxed, let any feelings you have buried come up to the surface, examine those feelings, decide which ones you want to keep and which ones you want to discard. Keep the ones you need right now and cast away the others. It is all right for you to feel sad or depressed sometimes. It is your way of being good to yourself. Depression is a healing process so you can allow yourself to mourn or be sad and when you have completed the time of sadness, set yourself free. You are good to yourself and the time will soon be over for those feelings and you will feel free from them. You will feel free because you can accept or discard any feelings you are through with. They are yours, and you can let them come and go, come and go as you need them. Now relax and continue to relax and feel yourself relaxed with your feelings, and think of how you are a whole person with many feelings that make you whole and healthy, and if any unwanted outside pressure comes at you, you are surrounded by a shield that protects you from pressure. The shield will protect you from pressure. The shield prevents outside pressure from invading you. Pressure bounces off and away from you, bounces off and away. No matter where it comes from, or who sends it, it just bounces off and away. It bounces off and away. You feel fine because the shield protects you all day from stress and pressure. You go through your day feeling fine. You watch the stress bounce off and away. The more stress outside the calmer you feel inside. The calmer you feel inside. You are a calm person and you are shielded from stress. You act in ways that make you feel good. You now have new responses to old situations. This new response will make you feel strong and calm and free. Your days will be full of accomplishments and you will be pleased with those accomplishments. You will feel good about yourself because you have new responses that are making your day more pleasant, you are calm and strong and free from stress. You are completely free from stress. You are free of all stress.

(Terminate trance or continue reinforcement)

Sleep Enhancement Intervention

This intervention should be adequate for patients that present with problems sleeping. Start this intervention at the medium state as you continue to pace the patient's breathing pattern.

Now just linger in your special place, there is no place to go, nothing to do. Just rest, just let yourself drift and float, drift and float into a sound and restful sleep, and as you drift deeper and deeper, visualize yourself lying in bed at night sleeping, notice how comfortable and relaxed you look...sleeping so soundly...appearing very comfortable, with no real effort when you go to bed every night, and as you lay there, I want you to think of nothing but the color blue...just let your thoughts fill with blue...and make sure you try to do this every night...before you finally let go...I know it will be difficult to experience nothing but the color blue, but I know you can do it for a while...so when my words come back to you, at night as you drift off to sleep...you will remember to try to stay awake, at least for a little while...to be aware of only the color blue...like the blue in the sky…or a robin's egg blue…or the deep blue sea…a beautiful calm blue, just the right shade of blue for you remembering to see only the color blue.

Improved Athletic Performance

This intervention is geared to assist the athlete in improving their performance in their chosen sport.

Start the intervention in the medium state and continue pacing the patient's breathing pattern.

Imagine preparing yourself for the challenge, your equipment is good and is adjusted to your needs, you are prepared both physically and mentally, now just imagine for a moment stressful situations that may arise…such as the weather, the actions of another player, or field conditions, and see yourself react to these conditions in a cool, undisturbed way. Now review in your mind your entire game (or sport) from start to finish, see it in slow motion…see it in as much detail as you can. Review all the strategy you used…this perfect game, your perfect game, can be played again and again, imagine yourself reaching your goal, you have reached your goal. You have reached this goal and you can go on to other goals whenever you like. Now just imagine how you felt during your perfect game, imagine that confidence and ease, you were focused and strong; imagine yourself begin again, take a few deep breaths and in slow motion see every action, feel every move in the most positive way. See yourself act and react, move perfectly, every muscle in harmony with your thought, see your strategy, see yourself moving perfectly, see every perfect move, and now notice how you feel, you feel relaxed, at ease, strong, alert, and clear-minded, your vision is sharp, your reflects are perfect, you feel great, now see yourself conclude and win the challenge, you feel pleased with yourself, and every correct move, every play is imprinted into your subconscious so that you can repeat your perfect game over and over like a film, now go back and once again replay the sequence in your mind, and this time at normal speed, imagine the sequence from start to finish…and see it in great detail, in the greatest of detail, imagine making all the right moves and playing a terrific game, the best game you ever played.

Depending on the sport, you will need to "tailor" the language to meet the needs of the patient. Reinforcement is good; try using a cassette tape with this intervention.

THE ULTIMATE INTERVENTION, SELF-HYPNOSIS

The most powerful intervention you can introduce a patient to is self-hypnosis. What makes self-hypnosis so powerful is that the patient owns it and takes responsibility for making it work. It is essentially capitalizing on the idea that the patient will progress better when he is empowered.

Self-hypnosis has to be the ultimate intervention for empowering our patients. Not all chemically dependent patients will respond well to using self-hypnosis. Those patients in the very early stages of recovery may not be ready or willing to assume responsibility for utilizing self-hypnosis. If they remain in recovery past the compliance phase to acceptance, they will become prime candidates to learn and practice self-hypnosis. Those patients who are obviously still stuck in denial or in compliance phase would not be good candidates to learn and practice self-hypnosis.

The patient needs to be made aware that self-hypnosis is not an "instant cure", but a powerful intervention that will work for them over time and with practice if you have done much hypnotic work with the patients. Then they will become excellent candidates to learn and utilize self-hypnosis because they already have a point of reference as to what it feels like to be in trance. By sensitizing your patient to trance you can expedite their motivation and training in self-hypnosis.

On the following pages you will find all the necessary information to train your patients in the use of self-hypnosis. First we list what needs to be known to formulate effective suggestions for the patient to use in their self-administered trance. From there we go on to a wide variety of self-hypnotic inductions.

Now it becomes a matter of selecting which self-hypnotic induction best fits your patient's model of the world.

Auto Suggestion
(Self-Hypnosis)

The suggestion is actually the sole agent of hypnosis and the exclusive means of behavior modification. When a person suggests thoughts and ideas to himself, he has already reasoned them out and has faith in them. Even in hetro-hypnosis the suggestions of the hypnotist do not take effect without the unconscious agreement of the subject.

We know that whenever there is a clash between the conscious and unconscious minds, it is the unconscious mind that wins out. Therefore, for a suggestion to be carried out by the conscious mind, acceptance by the unconscious mind is necessary. It follows that autosuggestion is usually much more meaningful than suggestions administered by some one else. Moreover, when a person gives suggestions to himself he will in fact participate directly and more actively in his behavior modification goals than when induced to do so by another person.

The most effective method of autosuggestion is probably a combination of pre-hypnotic and pictorial suggestions. The person will word his suggestion after meeting the preparatory conditions, and before self-hypnosis. When he has achieved self-hypnosis his visual image will reflect his suggestion.

In conveying suggestions to the unconscious mind picture images seem to be more effective than words. This is because the unconscious mind understands pictures better than words. A picture is, indeed, worth a thousand words!

If the patient can visualize himself doing a certain behavior or accomplishing something, then he becomes fully capable of accomplishing that scene. Normally it is not difficult for the patient to visualize himself doing a certain behavior as it usually is a behavior that at some point in their past was a normal behavior for him. Some patients may need to struggle harder than others to put together a picture(s) of themselves doing that desired behavior, but if you encourage them to endure the struggle the payoff will be well worth the effort. Your encouragement will be most instrumental in their beginning.

Deepening Procedures for Self-Hypnosis

Although light to deep trance has the same effect for the unconscious mind to assimilate the autosuggestion, to deepen autohypnosis a number of techniques can be applied, some of which are common to hetro-hypnosis.

Visual Imagery Technique: This is one of the best techniques for deepening self-hypnosis. You imagine yourself in any situation that gives you peace and serenity. For instance you may see yourself lying down comfortably in your bed, enjoying a sound sleep and pleasant dreams, or you may be lying in a hammock, or lying on a beach and watching the ocean waves or any similar relaxing imagery, "As you imagine drifting deeper into relaxation".

Escalator Technique: You may imagine yourself riding down an escalator. Then you start counting slowly to yourself from twenty to zero. You should think to yourself that the further the escalator goes down, the deeper you go into hypnosis. Also between each number you may imagine yourself drifting deeper into relaxation.

Counting Method: You may count from 100 forwards or backwards, and by one's, two's, three's, four's, etc. With every count you should imagine yourself drifting deeper and deeper into relaxation. Deepening self-hypnosis requires the same kind of practice or conditioning as the induction of hypnosis. Therefore, with every count you should coordinate your bodily functioning with your thoughts. For instance you should designate a particular number by which time you feel your mind is separated from your body.

Hand Levitation Method: You may suggest hand levitation to yourself and imagine that when your fingers touch your face, your arm will immediately become heavy and fall to your thigh. As this happens you will go deeper into hypnosis than ever before.

Post-Hypnotic Suggestion: As with hetro-hypnosis each time you hypnotize yourself you can give the suggestion that the next time you attempt self-hypnosis you will go more quickly and more deeply into the hypnotic state.

Deepening self-hypnosis can also be assisted by making a cassette tape.

RULES OF AUTO-SUGGESTION

For autosuggestions to be more effective a number of rules should be followed;

1. Suggestions should be condensed, revised, and perfected on a piece of paper and read several times prior to the induction of self-hypnosis.

2. Autosuggestions should be direct, permissive, and positive. Negative words and phrases such as "not", can't", "won't", should be avoided. Example: For a headache "Upon awakening, my headache will be gone." It would be better to suggest, "My head is feeling clear and better, I am becoming more and more comfortable and tranquil in every way." Another advantage of applying this procedure is that the unconscious mind will be given sufficient time to assimilate the idea.

3. The suggestion should be combined with a motive that enhances the effectiveness of the suggestion. This may be done through visual

imagery. Example: When a person gives himself a suggestion to overcome tension at the time of a job interview he may envision getting a good, prestigious job instead of saying to himself not to be nervous and tense during the interview.

4. Suggestions should be given singularly. The unconscious mind cannot deal with more than one idea at a time. Additionally, the suggestion should be repeated and reinforced in successive hypnotic sessions until the desired goal is achieved.

5. Auto-suggestions should be positively and logically worded and capable of being fulfilled.

In summation, the suggestion needs to be positive, short, (one to three sentences) and linked to a positive mental image as a point of reference for the patient's subconscious. Self-hypnosis can be done several times during an average day, but remember to deal with only one issue per trance to gain the maximum effectiveness of self-hypnosis. It is acceptable to do three separate self-hypnotic inductions and deal with three separate issues, but I recommend keeping your focus on just one issue until you have an acceptable resolution.

WAKING FROM SELF-HYPNOSIS

To awaken from self-hypnosis, (or more properly termed, to return to one's normal state of awareness) all you have to do is to suggest that you are going to do just that. This can be done in several ways.

1. Suggest to yourself that on the count of three you will be wide-awake, refreshed, and full of energy.

2. Envision the face of a clock set at the time you wish to awaken.

3. Think about the length of time you wish to remain in trance (this should be done prior to self-hypnosis), and the specific time you wish to wake up.

When you first start practicing self-hypnosis you may drop off into a natural sleep. To avoid this you can suggest to yourself that you will count back from 0 to 20, and at the count of 20 you will be in trance. Once you have achieved the hypnotic state and after you have accomplished auto-suggestion, you should count from 1 to 5, and at the count of 5 you will wake up.

When you are about to wake up always suggest to yourself that upon awaking you will feel relaxed, refreshed, clearheaded, full of energy, and happy.

SPIEGEL'S TECHNIQUE

This is another method of how to teach patients to hypnotize themselves and reinforce their therapeutic suggestions. This technique was developed by two brothers who were psychiatrists, Herbert and David Spiegel.

You should advise your patients to do the following. Sit or lie down and to yourself you count to three. At one, you do one thing, at two, you do two things, at three, and you do three things. In all, you carry out six things. At one look up towards your eyebrows, at two, while looking up, close your eyelids and take a deep breath, at three exhale, let your eyes relax and let your body float.

As you feel yourself floating you permit one hand or the other to feel like a buoyant balloon and let it float upwards. When it reaches this upright position it becomes a signal for you to enter a state of meditation.

This floating sensation signals your mind to turn inward and pay attention to your own thoughts. Like private meditation ballet dancers and athletes float all the time, that is why they concentrate and coordinate their movements so well. When they do not float they are tense and do not do as well.

Then the Spiegels advise their patients that in the beginning they should do these exercises as often as ten different times a day, preferably every one or two hours. At first the exercise takes a minute, but as the patient becomes more experienced he can do it in much less time.

According to the Spiegels, for the patient to de-hypnotize himself he should count backwards in this manner: Now three, get ready, two, with your eyelids closed, roll up your eyes, and one, let your eyelids open slowly. Then when your eyes are back in focus, slowly make a fist with the hand that is up, and as you open your fist slowly, your usual sensation and control returns, let your hand float downwards.

This is a version that requires practice several times over to master.

Subjective Technique

Sit in a comfortable chair or lie down on a couch or bed. Fix your eyes on a spot on the wall above eye level or on the ceiling. Try to meet all the preparatory requirements for self-hypnosis. Then focus your attention on your eyelids. During the procedure think of the symbol "55".

Now, first imagine that your eyelids are becoming very heavy. Try to feel this heaviness. Again and again tell yourself mentally; "My eyes are getting very heavy". I feel my eyes getting very heavy, and the heavier they become, the more comfortable and relaxed I feel. It seems that it is impossible for me to keep my eyelids open. It really feels so good to close my eyes. I am going count to three. When I complete the count, it will be absolutely impossible for me to keep my eyes open. One, my eyes are narrowing to a slit, they are about to close. Two, my eyelids are going to drop involuntarily. Three, they are closing…they are closing, they are closing. (Now tell yourself) "My eyelids are now locked together, they are stuck fast, so tightly that I can not open them. Now, do not try any longer. I can open my eyes when ever I choose, but will keep them closed for the remainder of the induction." Now think of a peaceful scene. Imagine you are walking around a swimming pool in the middle of a beautiful garden. It is spring, the weather is very pleasant. It is 3 o'clock in the afternoon; you keep walking alongside the pool. All around the pool are red, white and yellow roses. Alongside the pool are jasmine trees. A mild breeze blows from the flowers, bringing the sweet smell of roses and jasmine. As you continue walking, the sweet jasmine scent stays with you. Suddenly, a few yards from the pool, you see a hammock stretched between two shady trees. You decide to lie down in that hammock in the midst of the beautiful garden and enjoy a deep relaxation. So, you approach the hammock, you lie down in it, and find it very comfortable and relaxing. You feel so relaxed and comfortable that ten minutes of actual time pass like one minute. As you enjoy your relaxed state, a pretty bird lands on the branch of a tree in front of you. You keep looking at it. After a few seconds the bird leaves its perch and starts to fly toward you. It is getting closer and closer to you. You wish to follow the movements of the bird, but the beauty of the scene causes you to close your eyes and go into a very deep sleep.

This imagery may work as a very pleasant method of induction and take you into a deep hypnotic trance. Any variation of this scene which suits individual needs can be applied for the induction of self-hypnosis. You may even tape a scene like the above and listen to it.

COMBINATION TECHNIQUE

Seat yourself in a comfortable chair with your feet flat on the floor and your legs extended and your hands on your thighs or on the arms of the chair. Meet the preparatory rules for self-hypnosis. Fix your gaze on something above eye level.

Begin counting slowly from 1 to 10. Say the number one, direct your attention on your eyes and tell yourself repeatedly, "My eyes are getting heavy, very heavy. I feel my eyes becoming so heavy at the count of 3 I will not be able to keep them open, they will close automatically". Count to two and think of the symbol "55". Roll your eyes up into the back of your head, then count to three and tell yourself, "My eyelids are so heavy now that I cannot open them. It is just as if they were glued together. I will now go deeper into self-relaxation. I am able to open my eyes whenever I choose, but I will keep them closed for the remainder of the induction. Next, count to 4, think of the symbol "55", and give yourself the following suggestions: My toes, feet, calves, and legs are getting very heavy. I feel a tingling sensation all over my legs. It feels very nice. Both my legs, from my toes up to the pelvic area feel stuck to the floor. I now go even deeper into self.-relaxation. I am able to move my legs whenever I choose, and I now will go even deeper into self-relaxation. Now count to 5, think of the "55" and say to yourself: I feel my abdominal muscles becoming numb and heavy. Even the pit of my stomach is becoming wooden-like and relaxed. Count to 6, think of the image "55", and continue telling yourself: "Now I can feel the muscles in my chest becoming relaxed, I am breathing more regularly and more easily. (Then thinking now and then of the symbol-"55", continue counting and with the count of 7, tell yourself): "Now I feel a numb, wooden-like sensation in my fingers, wrists, hands, arms and forearms. My arms feel just as though I have been sleeping on them. Eight, the muscles of my neck and my entire body, from my neck down, are relaxed. Nine, I feel my facial muscles becoming loose. My head is also very heavy and at the same time very relaxed and refreshed. My whole body feels loose and limp, from the top of my head right down to my toes. With every breath I take I can feel myself drifting into a deeper and deeper state of relaxation. Then you have to visualize a relaxed and pleasant scene like the one described in the "Subjective Technique". It can be some pleasant scene you imagine in the future. It can be a peaceful, mountainous scene, a blue sky with one or two billowy clouds moving slowly. On a lake with a sailboat floating gently, or any scene that makes you feel good, drowsy, and relaxed.

The "key word" and suggestions should be given at the appropriate time. The more practice you put into this procedure will be directly reflected in the outcome you achieve. This would be an excellent script to record on a cassette for your personal use.

DEEP MUSCLE RELAXATION TRAINING

This is phase one of three phases. The Muscle Relaxation Phase and Guided Imagery Phase follows this script and should be taught in this order. This is particularly good for your patients who have trouble relaxing. The number of seconds to pause is denoted by the number in parentisis (8).

Welcome to this session, during the next 30 minutes we will work our way through deep muscle relaxation training. The end result of this session is for you to have a heightened sense of awareness of what your body feels like to be fully relaxed. This technique alone will not teach you every thing you need to know. It is imperative that you practice all three phases of this program.

We will begin by having you assume a comfortable position. You can either be sitting down in a chair or lying down. If you use a chair, try to make it one with arms, if lying down, do not use a pillow. If your clothing is too tight and uncomfortable, loosen it slightly now (4). Settle back now as comfortable as you can (4). Focus your attention on my voice (3). As other thoughts drift into your mind, let them drift away and continue to focus on my voice only (4). (Spend four minutes talking the client through a deep breathing exercise). As you relax, clench your right fist, now clench your fist tighter and tighter, and study the tension in your right fist and forearm. You can feel the tension become uncomfortable in your right fist and forearm. You can feel the tension become uncomfortable in your right fist as you keep it tightly clenched (3). Now relax (4). Let the fingers of your right hand become loose (5). Observe the contrast in the feelings of your right hand (5). Let yourself go and try to become more relaxed all over (5). Once more again, clench your right fist really tight (3). Hold it tight (3). Now notice the tension again, it feels very tight and uncomfortable (2). Now let go (2). Relax, straighten out your fingers (3). Notice the difference once more (10). Now we will repeat that with your left hand and forearm (2). Clench your left fist while the rest of your body relaxes (3). Clench your fist tight and feel the tension (3). Now relax (5). Again, enjoy the contrast in feelings (4). Let your mind focus on that feeling of relaxation. Repeat that once more; clench your left fist (3). Make your fist very tight and tense (3). Now relax and feel the difference (4). Slowly straighten out your fingers (10). Clench both fists now (3). Tight, and tighter (2). Both fists tense, forearms tense, study the sensation (2). Relax now (2). Let the feelings of relaxation flow into both hands (2). Straighten out your fingers and feel the relaxation (3). Continue relaxing your hands and forearms more and more (3). Now bend both your elbows and tense your biceps by pulling your hands towards your shoulders (3). Tense, them tighter and study the feelings of tension (5). Now straighten out your arms (4). Let them relax, and now feel the difference again (3). Let the relaxation develop (8). Once more, tense your biceps (4). Hold that tension and observe it carefully (4). Straighten your arms and allow the feelings of relaxation to flow into yours arms (4). Relax to the best of your ability (8). Now straighten your arms so that you feel the most tension in the triceps muscle along the back of your arms (3). Now relax (5). Move your arms back into a comfortable position (5). Let the relaxation flow on its own accord (8). Your arms should feel comfortably heavy as you allow the relaxation to flow (5). Once more, straighten your arms so that you feel the tension in your triceps (8). Let your arms relax again and focus on the comfortable heavy feeling of relaxation in your arms (6). Now let's focus on pure relaxation in the arms without any tension. Move your arms into a comfortable position and let them relax (8). Let the relaxation flow into your arms (3). Focus on that nice warm feeling in your arms (10). Even when your arms seem fully relaxed, try to let your arms achieve a deeper level of relaxation (12). Now we will move upwards to the head and shoulders (2). We will start by letting all your muscles go loose and heavy. Just settle back quietly and comfortably. Wrinkle up your forehead now (3). Wrinkle it tighter (5). Now stop wrinkling your forehead (4). Relax and allow it to smooth out (3). Picture your entire forehead and scalp becoming smoother as the relaxation increases (10). Now frown and crease your brows and study the tension (6). Let go of the tension once again, smooth out your forehead once more (10). Now close your eyes tighter and tighter (5). Feel the tension (3). Now relax your eyes (4). keep your eyes closed gently, comfortably and notice the relaxation (10). Now clench your jaws (10). Relax your jaws now, let your lips part slightly (6). Appreciate the feeling of relaxation (12). Now press your tongue hard against the roof of your mouth (4). Look for the tension (4). All right, let your tongue return to a comfortable and relaxed position (10). Now press your lips together (4). Tighter and tighter (4). Relax your lips; note the contrast between tension and relaxation (8). Feel the relaxation all over your face (8). Now to attend to your neck muscles, press your head back as far as it can go and feel the tension in your neck (3). Roll it to the right and feel the tension shift (3). Now roll it to the left (3). Straighten your head and bring it forward (3). Press your chin against your chest (4). Let your head return to a comfortable position, and study the relaxation (5). Let the relaxation develop (10). Now shrug your shoulders straight up (4). Hold the tension (4). Drop your shoulders slowly and feel the relaxation (4). Feel your neck and shoulders relaxing (8). Shrug your shoulders up and forward (4). Now back, Feel the tension in your shoulders and in your upper back (4). Drop your shoulders slowly once more and relax (6). Let the relaxation spread deeply into your shoulders, right into your back muscles (6). Relax your neck and throat, and your jaw and other facial areas as the pure relaxation takes over and goes deeper (3). Deeper, even deeper (10). Allow yourself to focus on the warm, heavy comfortable feeling in your face and shoulders (12). If other thoughts drift into your mind, let them drift on by and continue to focus on my voice (8). We now shift our focus to the trunk of your body, start with relaxing your entire body to the best of your ability (8). Feel that comfortable heaviness that accompanies relaxation (8). Breathe easily and freely, in and out (5). Notice how the relaxation increases as you exhale (10). As you breathe out, feel that relaxation (4). Now breathe in and fill tip your lungs, inhale deeply and hold your breath (4). Study the sensation (3). Now exhale, let the walls of your chest grow loose and push the air out automatically (3). Continue relaxing and breathe freely and gently (6). Feel the relaxation and enjoy it (8). With the rest of your body as relaxed as possible, fill your lungs again (8). That's fine breath out, and again, breathe in deeply and hold it (8). Now breathe out and appreciate the relief (4). Just breathe normally (6). Continuing relaxing your chest and let the relaxation spread to your back (6). To your shoulders (6). To your neck (6). To your arms (6). Merely let go and enjoy the relaxation (12). Now let's pay attention to your abdominal. muscles, pull your stomach in (3). Pull the muscles right in and feel the tension this way (6). Now relax again, let your stomach out. Continue to breathe normally and easily and feel the gentle massaging action all over your chest and stomach (12). Now pull your stomach in again and hold the tension (8). Release the tension (8). Once more pull in your stomach fully and feel the tension (8). Now relax your stomach fully (3). Let the tension dissolve as the relaxation grows deeper (6). Each time you breathe out notice the rhythmic relaxation both in your lungs and in your stomach (10). Notice how your chest and stomach relaxes more and more (8). Try and let go of all the muscle tension anywhere in your body (12). Now direct your attention to your lower back (3). Arch up your back, make your lower back quite hollow, and feel the tension along your spine (4). Now settle back comfortably again, relaxing the lower back (10). Arch your back up again and feel the tension as you do so. Try to keep the rest of your body relaxed as possible. Try to localize the tension throughout your lower back area (2). Relax once more (3). Relax your upper back (6). Spread the relaxation to your stomach (6). Now to your chest (6). Now to your shoulders (6). Now to your arms (6). Now to your facial area (6). These parts are relaxing father and father, and father and even deeper (6). Let it flow as a warm, heavy, comfortable feeling (1.2). Let go of all tensions and just relax (8). Now *flex* your buttocks and thighs. Flex your thighs by pressing down your heels as hard as you can (6). Relax and note the difference (8). Straighten your knees and flex your thigh muscles again, hold the tension (6). Relax your hips and thighs (8). Allow the relaxation to proceed on its own. (10). Press your feet and toes downwards, away from your face, so that calf muscles become tense, study that tension (6). Relax your feet and calves (8). This time, bend your feet away from your face so that you feel tension along your shins (6) bring your toes back up (2) relax again. (6) Keep relaxing for a while (6), now let yourself relax further all over (6). Relax your feet (6). Relax your ankles now (6). Relax your calves now (6). Relax your shins now (6). Relax your knees now (6). Relax your thighs now (6). Relax your buttocks now (6). Relax your hips now (6). Feel the heaviness of your lower body as you relax still further (8). Let go now, more and more (4). Feel that relaxation all over. Let it proceed to your upper back (6). Keep relaxing more and more deeply (12). Make sure that no tension has crept into your throat (2). Relax your neck and your jaws and all your facial muscles (4). Keep relaxing your whole body like that for a while. Let yourself totally relax (12). Now you can become twice as relaxed by taking in a really deep breath and slowly exhaling (6). Close your eyes so that you become less aware of objects and movements around you, and prevent any surface tensions from developing (8). Breathe in deeply and feel yourself becoming heavier (6). Take a long deep breath and let it out very slowly (6). Feel how heavy and relaxed you have become (12). The relaxation is flowing through you in a warm and comfortable way (30). In a state of perfect relaxation you should feel unwilling to move a single muscle in your body (3). Think about the effort that would be required to raise your right arm, as you think about raising your right arm, see if you can notice any tensions that might have crept into your right shoulder and your arm (6). Now you decide not to lift your arm, but to continue relaxing (12). Observe the relief and the disappearance of the tension (6). Just continue relaxing like that (12). When you wish to get up, count backward from five to one (6). You should then feel fine and refreshed, wide-awake and clam, slowly open your eyes and look about (4). Flex your fingers and toes slightly. Now in a slow and easy manner you can bring yourself to your feet (6). It maybe necessary for you to repeat this exercises several. times to develop a strong sense of awareness of what your body feels like to be relaxed. The value of this exercise is for you to develop a heightened sense of awareness of the feelings of relaxation, and the feelings of tension.

MUSCLE RELAXATION EXERCISE

Welcome to the second in a series of your relaxation training. Before moving into the second phase of this program lets take a minute to review the first phase. Hopefully by now, you have repeated the first phase of relaxation and tension. During this phase I want you to mentally recall the feelings you experienced during the first session. Recall it slowly (10). Tighten and loosen your muscles if needed to re-awaken the feeling of relaxation (10). Settle back, and make yourself comfortable (15). Also recall the breathing exercises now that we are prepared (15). Lets move on (5). Begin with your feet, focus on your toes and feet, focus on that comfortable, warm, heavy feeling (10). If you find distracting thoughts drift into your mind, let them drift on by, don't try to force the thoughts out of your mind (3). Just let them drift on by (10). Focus now on the calves of your legs (10). Feel them grow heavier and heavier (10). Feel the tension drift away and that heavy comfortable feeling flow in (15). Now let that nice feeling of relaxation flow slowly upwards (15). You can feel it slowly working into your thighs (10). You're now feeling that nice warm heavy feeling spread throughout your thighs (10). Feel your thigh grow heavier and heavier (10). Feel the tension drift away and that heavy comfortable feeling flow freely (15). If you find distracting thoughts coming into your mind, let them drift on by and continue to focus on my voice (15). Let that comfortable feeling move upwards into your hips and buttocks (10). Let that mental image become warm and heavy, very comfortable (15). The feeling is becoming very soothing and relaxing (15). The feeling becomes more and more comfortable as the tension drifts away (20). Now feel that comfortable feeling move up into your stomach and lower back (10). Feel the tension start slowly drift away (10). That comfortable feeling of relaxation is starting to flow in and feels so soothing and warm (10). The feeling of relaxation continues to grow and feel warmer and more comfortable (10). Don't hesitate to let your body relax and sink into a wonderful. Feeling of relaxation (15). It is now traveling Upwards again, into your chest and shoulders (8). The tension is now flowing away (10). The tension still slowly drifting (10). The feeling of relaxation is now taking over in your chest and shoulders (15). Spreading so slowly, and very relaxing (20). The feeling of relaxation becomes deeper and deeper (25). Now the feeling of relaxation is seeping down through your arms and into your hands (15). Now you feel your arms and hands grow warm and heavy (12). That heavy comfortable feeling is becoming more and more soothing (12). The tension has drifted out of arms and hands now, and the warm heavy feeling is flowing freely (10). Your arms and hands continue to grow warm and heavy (10). Let the feeling of relaxation go deeper and deeper (20). Now let your mind slowly move to focus on your neck and scalp (15). Let the warm comfortable feeling spread up through your neck and into your scalp (10). The tension. is slowly drifting away (12). Now the warm comfortable feeling is flowing and feeling better and better (12). Slowly you feel the warmth move you deeper and deeper into relaxation (15). The feeling of relaxation is now drifting down into your facial muscles (10). The tension is drifting out now and that warm relaxed feeling is increasing (15). Now the warm heavy comfortable feeling if flowing with warmth and comfort (30). Now you are feeling that warm, heavy, comfortable feeling engulf your entire body (45). The feeling flows so freely into the warm wonderful feeling of relaxation (60). Now, very Slowly count backwards from five to one (10). Now slowly move, your toes (5). Now also move your fingers slightly (5). Open your eyes and slowly look about you (4). At this time you wi11 start to feel more alert and refreshed (6). You may feet free to get up now and move about.

It is recommended that you practice this technique several times before moving on to the guided imagery phase.

GUIDED IMAGERY

During this session we will focus on guided imagery as a means of relaxation. This is the third and final teaching phase in progressive relaxation techniques. We start this session with a reflective look back to the sessions of deep muscle techniques and muscle relaxation. Try to recall in your mind the feelings you experienced during these exercises. The number in parentheses (0) denote pauses in seconds.

Assume a comfortable position before you begin to form the mental image of your body relaxing (6). Loosen any tight clothing and let the warm comfortable feeling of relaxation take over (12). If any distracting thoughts enter your mind, let them drift on bye and continue to focus on the sound of my voice, and that warm, heavy and comfortable feeling that is starting to move through your body (15). If you have trouble recalling that feeling of relaxation at this time, stop briefly and perform phase one again of the deep muscle relaxation technique until you have developed a re-awareness of relaxation in your body (15). Now mentally recreate that feeling of relaxation in your body (10). Let it begin with your toes (10). Slowly, that warm comfortable feeling starts moving upwards (10). Now moving into the calves of your legs (10). The warm heavy feeling is flowing stronger, but quite easily (15). The feeling now moves into your thighs (10). Slowly and very warmly spreading (10). That warm comfortable feeling is now moving into your hips and buttocks (10). Slowly and warmly the feeling of relaxation is spreading throughout your lower body (10). Feel the warmth and comfort spread to your stomach and lower back (10). Feel those muscles gently let go and the relaxation flow in (15). The warm feeling of comfort is now spreading upwards through your chest and shoulders (10). Progressing gently and slowly onwards up through your neck and scalp (15). Take a. minute now to dwell on the feeling you are experiencing in your body. (Sixty-second pause) Now that you have achieved a state of relaxation, continue to focus on my voice as we create a mental picture in your mind (10). Imagine yourself now, sitting down and leaning against a huge tree in an open field (15). You are sitting in lush soft green grass (15). You can feel a gentle warm breeze (10). The breeze is soft and warm on your face (15). Just like a soft warm caress (15). You feel very relaxed now, deeply relaxed (10). A warm comfortable feeling holds your body and mind in relaxation (15). In your mind's eye you slowly turn and look upwards (5). Looking to the top of the tree filled with leaves (10). You see that warm gentle breeze stirring the leaves on the tree, ever so softly and gently (10). You casually notice that from the top of the tree a leaf has broken away and is starting to fall (10). The warm breeze is cradling the leaf (10). Rocking the leaf gently back and forth (10). The leaf moves ever so slowly in the breeze (10). Feel that warm gentle breeze again, gently touching your face (10). Notice the free flowing relaxation going through your body (15). You also notice that the leaf is still falling ever so slowly (10). It is still being cradled and rocked, back and forth by the gentle warm breeze you feel (15). The leaf is still slowly working its way down in its descent to the ground (15). The leaf is moving so slowly and unhurried

(15). Still gently floating and moving so gracefully with the breeze (15). Unhurried or bothered by time, the leaf continues its slow and deliberate descent to the ground (15). Let your mind slowly turn inward to become re-aware of the wonderful state of relaxation your body is enjoying (20). That comfortable, warm heavy feeling continues to flow through out your person (30). Now your mind slowly turns back to the leaf (5). It is still making its graceful descent downwards (15). Still gently swaying in the breeze (10). Back and forth, so slowly and gently, as it moves to its downward destination (15). With slow graceful motion the warm pleasant breeze you feel is still carrying the leaf father downward (15). You observe the leaf moving with gentle and tender grace (15). The leaf is being cradled by the warm breeze, you can also feel the warmness of your body relaxing, and the gentle warm breeze caressing you (20). The leaf is moving slowly (10). Still making its unhurried descent to the ground below (20). The leaf is coming closer to the ground now (15). Still gently and slowly moving with an air of grace in its every movement (20). At times the leaf will appear almost to be suspended in the air by the gentle nurturing of the warm breeze (20). Now it appears to be in its final, but graceful descent (20). Slowly, with a gentle swaying motion, the leaf comes to rest beside you (10). The leaf, like you, has finally come to a complete state of rest. Mentally let your mind explore your body in this state of relaxation (60). Now slowly count backwards from five to one (10). Slowly now, open your eyes and look about you (5). Slowly move your toes and fingers, and you will find muscle tension returning (10).

To obtain the maximum amount of effectiveness from these sessions it is recommended that you repeat this exercise several. times over on your own. In time the mental image of the falling leaf will become your key to unlocking your relaxation through, your mind's association with this mental image. You may in the future decide to create your own. personal image to better suit your personality. I would recommend you consult with an individual in the field of psychology for assistance and guidance.

If you do not desire to seek out consultation, I would suggest you use a serene, calm scene for your mental image, such as a lake, snow covered mountain, etc.

OUTPATIENT TREATMENT MODEL

This outpatient treatment model probably does not vary greatly from the accepted norm for chemical dependency treatment. The first several pages will generally outline the program, and then I will offer specific treatment possibilities using clinical hypnotherapy.

Unfortunately, many chemical dependency outpatient treatment facilities are money driven and overregulated by the state they operate in. With these two given situations, effective treatment for the individual patient is often over looked in an effort to comply with all the regulations that were designed to help and protect the patient. What a Catch-22! Regulations have their place in society, but as with many state agencies there seems to be rule makers that continue to pump out excessive regulations to create job security and attempt to look like they are doing a great job, when in fact they continue to "gum up" the treatment systems.

With other agencies there are definite problems with counselors and therapists who are always driving down a pre-canned treatment system as fast as they can to hurry up and produce the almighty dollars. There is no fast or easy solution for the ills of the treatment centers. As long as chemical dependency treatment is in vogue, there seems to be adequate public funding, but now chemical dependency treatment is starting to fall out of fashion in our nation.

Solution: More self-help treatment made available to the general public at a low cost with faster results. While this could be possible, I doubt seriously that it will ever take place on a large scale, mainly because as soon as the large money players in chemical dependency treatment find out, they will mount a campaign to stop it. Consider the overall treatment proposed here, and pick and choose what you can incorporate in your treatment system.

Adult Intensive Outpatient Program

This program is specifically designed for the treatment of alcohol abuse, alcoholism and other drug abuse. The nature of these problems is complex and diverse and therefore. requires a multi-faceted approach to successful treatment.

In order to effectively address the issues of addiction and the disease concept of alcoholism the objective of the Adult Intensive Out-Patient Program will be to provide a concentrated out-patient program consisting of a combination of educational sessions and couples programs. Whenever possible the client's family or a social support system will be involved in the treatment process.

All clients and their families shall be encouraged to participate in A.A/N.A/ALANON and related programs in addition to the treatment sessions. Urinalysis tests and Antabuse will also be used as adjuncts to therapy when necessary.

The outpatient program will focus on total abstinence and freedom from chemical dependency. The first six weeks of treatment will consist of group therapy sessions, three hours per day, four days a week. Individual counseling sessions will be in addition to the group therapy for a total of 72 hours of treatment services. Clients will also be required to attend one A.A/ self-help support group meeting per week. During the individual counseling sessions the counselor will review the client's treatment progress and note it in the client's case file. Each Client will receive an individual counseling session at least once within every twenty hours of treatment and additionally as needed.

Class size will be limited to twelve clients per counselor. The length of time each client spends in the program past the minimum requirements will depend on the client's progress based on staff evaluation.

Each client will have an individual treatment plan that is designed to meet their own unique problems and needs and to help them understand their alcohol/drug problems. This shall be accomplished by taking into account all case history and diagnostic information. The initial treatment plan must be prepared within 21 days of admission or by the third visit, whichever is earlier. The treatment plan shall include:

A. Specific problems to be addressed.
B. Objectives to be accomplished in treating the problem.
C. Anticipated length of treatment and time linked means to be used in achieving the client's objectives.

Admission Criteria: Screening criteria shall include diagnostic techniques as needed to assure the appropriateness of placement in the intensive outpatient mode. The diagnosis at a minimum shall include an assessment by a, qualified counselor of the client's progression in the disease determined by using the characteristics/symptoms as mentioned from both the progression chart and the diagnostic interview results sheet. Clients that demonstrate at least three symptoms from either list or combined will be considered appropriate for intensive outpatient treatment, given the progressive nature of chemicals dependency.

Progression Evaluation Chart

All clients wi11 be assessed as one of the following:

1. No significant problem

2. Early stage problem

3. Middle/late stage

A. No significant problem
   Any client not showing using symptomology as listed below will
   assessed as NSP. Clients with more than one DWI in a five-year period.
B. Early stage problem

Clients showing the following signs/symptoms will be assessed as early stage.
Periodic or occasional blackouts.
Increased tolerance.
Hurried ingestion of chemicals.
Legal problems due to consumption.
Sneaking drinks.
Increased use or preoccupation.
No loss of control reported.

C. Middle stage problem

Clients showing the following wi11 be assessed as middle stage users.

Loss of control.
Periods of abstinence.
Criticized by significant others.
Alibis.

Guilt/Remorse.
Legal problems related to alcohol/drugs.
Regular blackouts.
Geographical escape.
Protecting supply.
No medical complications reported.

D. Late stage problem

Clients showing the following signs and symptoms will be assessed as late stage.

Tremors.
Alcohol /drug related medical complaints.
Decreased tolerance.
Indefinable fears.
Withdrawal syndrome.
Ethical deterioration.

DWI clients will be considered appropriate for the intensive outpatient program. If other diagnostic impressions, family conferences and intake/diagnostic interviews deemed treatment appropriate.

The motivation for recovery and the ability to attain and maintain abstinence on an outpatient basis shall be indicated at a minimum by the client's willingness to enter and attend all scheduled treatment sessions as described above in the program description for intensive outpatient treatment. Scheduled sessions missed by the client must be documented either by a physician's statement or an employer's statement requiring the client to meet an unusual work schedule. Otherwise the client must attend all scheduled sessions.

Although relapse can be part of the addiction process, continued use of mood-altering chemicals. Unless prescribed by a physician, shall, not be permitted and the client shall be dismissed from the program and referred the intensive inpatient treatment after consultation with the Clinical Director.

Social Support Systems: The client's current living situation should be stable. The client should be employed, or employable and actually seeking employment, the client's ability to finance their intensive outpatient program must be considered for his suitability for intensive outpatient treatment. It is suggested, but not required that a client's family or significant other participate in the program. Physical health and general mental health. Should the client or the counselor notice any physical limitations to attending intensive outpatient treatment, the client will be referred to his physician for an exam and a medical release prior to starting treatment. Should any mental difficulties be noticed, the client will be referred to the community mental health for an exam and a release prior to starting treatment.

Clients that do not meet the above listed criteria will not be placed in intensive outpatient treatment. Before a client is considered officially enrolled in the intensive out-patient program, he must;

1. Complete the intake/diagnostic process.

2. Sign and be given a copy of the program rules and guidelines.

3. Sign consent to treat.

4. Complete financial commitment.

Client discharge and transfer: Should a client who is enrolled in the intensive outpatient program be unable to complete the program he will be considered for transfer to an inpatient facility. This will be determined by the client, counselor and clinical director. Reasons for this transfer are, but not limited to: Relapses, personal, family, work, and health problems. Every effort will be made to ensure a smooth transition to the new program ensuring that the client's best interests are maintained.

Should a client be unable to successfully complete the program and not wish to transfer, he will be discharged from the program. All courts will be sent a discharge summary notifying them that the client failed to successfully complete the program. A copy of the discharge summary will become a permanent part of the client's file, and the client will receive a copy.

Program Completion: Upon successful completion of the intensive outpatient treatment program the client will be referred to a structured aftercare program. All courts will be sent a discharge summary notifying them of the client's successful completion of a program. A copy of the discharge summary will become a permanent part of the client's case file and the client will receive a copy.

ADULT INTENSIVE OUT-PATIENT PROGRAM DESCRIPTION

The intensive outpatient program is six weeks in length for adult alcoholics or chemically dependent patients. It is designed as an alternative to in-patient treatment for clients who are:

1. In the early to middle to stages of addiction.

2. Employed.

3. Have a sufficient social support base.

4. Do not have physical/emotional/mental impairment.

5. Have the ability to attain and maintain abstinence on an outpatient basis.

The objectives of the program are:
To maintain abstinence.

To provide the client and his significant other with education regarding chemical dependency and recovery.

To increase the client's support base through participation in A.A/N.A/ALANON/ etc.

To provide the client and his significant other with counseling through the first six weeks of abstinence.

To provide the client and his significant others with skills and resources to address and resolve problems.

To assist the client in designing a plan and aftercare plan to maintain abstinence.

Admission is conducted in two steps:

The first step is to obtain an evaluation and assessment of the client's involvement with alcohol and other drugs and to determine the appropriateness of the referral. The second step is to determine if the client and his significant other meets the intensive outpatient criteria.

Upon admission, the client and his significant other will be assigned to a qualified counselor who will provide all their individual and family counseling services throughout the program. Individual counseling sessions lasting one hour each will be required per every twenty hours of treatment and additionally as needed. A family session will be held once monthly for one hour.

The program consists of seventy-two hours of education, individual, group and family counseling for the client. The client is also required to attend six meetings of A.A/N.A/ALANON, etc. The client's significant other is provided twenty-eight hours of educational and counseling services. The significant other is strongly encouraged to attend six meetings of Al-anon.

Upon satisfactory completion of program requirements the client will be discharged from the intensive outpatient program and referred to a structured aftercare program.

Two Year Out-Patient Program

Intensive outpatient, Phase 1

Six weeks, four days per week, Monday through Thursday, 6pm to 9pm. Client is a]-so seen individually per every twenty hours of treatment services. Each group session will be educational in nature with group processing.

Aftercare, Phase 2

Once weekly group sessions each. Friday from 6pm to 7:30pm for a period of six months, (twenty four group sessions). Once monthly individual sessions are required, more sessions are encouraged.

Maintained, Phase 3

Once monthly group sessions on the last Friday of each month from 6pm to 7:30pm for approximately sixteen months to program completion. Once monthly individual. sessions are required.

Support Groups

Throughout the entire two-year program all clients are required to attend at least one A.A/N.A. support type group meeting. Each client will maintain a log to be signed at each meeting to be signed by the individual chairing the meeting. All completed logs will be kept in the client's case file.

Aftercare Program Description

Purpose:

The Aftercare Program is designed to move the Client through a further phase of recovery by assisting the client to assume responsibility and management of his own recovery and to guide the client in identifying the. obstacles to achieving self-managed recovery, and to assist the client in developing tools to have a drug-free lifestyle.

OBJECTIVES:

The objectives of this group are to help the client:

1. Become aware of feelings/emotions which were suppressed or ignored while in the disease process of alcoholism.

2. Examine defense mechanisms and develop alternative responses to relate more positively.

3. Develop a more positive self-image in recovery.

4. Develop an on-going monitoring process to identify relapse cues and develop plans to deal with relapse prevention.

5. Complete the process of self-examination through the use of the 4th and 5th steps of A.A.

6. Assist the client to develop a clean &. sober lifestyle.

7. Develop a viable support system in A.A. & group members.

8. Help the client learn healthier and more beneficial ways of coping with stress. Relaxation and Meditation

9. Teach the client good nutrition in recovery.

10. Assist the client in planning.

11. Assist the client and family members in adjusting to the changing dynamics of the in the family.

Admission Criteria:

The admission criteria for the aftercare program are:

1. Successful completion of an intensive alcohol/drug treatment program. (IOP or In-Patient)

2. Continued sobriety since their completion of the intensive phase of treatment.

3. Personal interview with the aftercare counselor.

4. Clients who have previous group experience or who have enjoyed a period of sobriety through A.A/N.A may be admitted into the aftercare group. This will be based on the aftercare counselor's discretion.

Description & Length of Aftercare:

Aftercare group will. meet once weekly from 6pm to 7:30pm. Average length of stay in aftercare is six months.

Discharge Criteria

1. Completion of 24 group sessions.

2. Consistently maintaining sobriety.

3. Attendance of once weekly A.A/N.A meetings, 24 meetings.

4. Active participation in the group process.

5. Fulfilling all financial responsibilities with the treatment center.

This treatment model. would have the early stage patients in the program for one year and the middle and late stage patients attending for the full two years. Here again this is just a generic treatment model which could be built upon to meet the needs of the patients and the local regulatory agencies.

With this outline of a proposed chemical dependency outpatient treatment program it is easy to see all. the possible areas to incorporate the use of clinical hypnotherapy. Any possible phase of treatment could be enhanced by the use of clinical hypnotherapy. The difference between standard interventions and hypnotic interventions is like comparing the difference between white glue and super glue in relation to the "sticking" power of the interventions.

The group process is another useful area for ethical hypnotherapy. If the group members are also the patients you see individually you have an automatic advantage as these group members are already sensitized to trance. Doing trance work in group also puts aside the problem of having group members operating at different levels at the same time with the group members under the influence of hypnosis Issues still can be addressed and information taught. Group hypnosis is an ideal setting to work on broad issues like self-esteem, motivation, behaviors, etc.

In closing I hope this book will serve you well as a desktop reference, ready to serve you this information. The interventions listed in this book are quite effective as they are and I would encourage you to change and modify these interventions to serve the needs of your patients. There is so much good we can provide for our patients if we are creative and willing to use the information that is at our disposal.

ABOUT THE AUTHOR

Randy Hartman has recieved his Masters Degree in Human Relations from the University of Oklahoma. Randy has also written four other books on the subject of clinical hypnosis.He has also served as a chemical dependency counselor, mental health therapist and clinical hypnotherapist.

Lightning Source UK Ltd.
Milton Keynes UK
06 October 2009

144632UK00001B/109/A